Best wishes
David Whitehead
24· ii ·1983

YESTERDAY'S TOWN: HEREFORD

FRONT COVER: Church Street, seen here at the beginning of the century, is one of the few streets to have retained its character unaltered. Tourists have been visiting the City for centuries. Hence, Church Street, even then, had its fair share of antique and curiosity shops. Viscount Torrington was excited by the quarto volume of plays and poems he bought here from a second-hand bookseller in 1787. One perhaps regrets the disappearance of the Caxton Press, the Gardeners Arms and Mr Thistleton, the umbrella mender, but the present diversity of shops is equally attractive. Even the signs, with the help of Conservation Area legislation, have remained consistent. Only the two 'cottages' in the foreground — to use the classless euphemism of the directories — have disappeared.

A country town photographer: William Henry Bustin and Son, Palace Yard c1890.

YESTERDAY'S TOWN:
HEREFORD

BY

DAVID WHITEHEAD

BARRACUDA BOOKS LIMITED
BUCKINGHAM, ENGLAND
MCMLXXXIII

PUBLISHED BY BARRACUDA BOOKS LIMITED
BUCKINGHAM, ENGLAND
AND PRINTED BY
BLACKWELL'S IN THE CITY OF
OXFORD, ENGLAND

BOUND BY
WOOLNOUGH BOOKBINDING
WELLINGBOROUGH, ENGLAND

JACKET PRINTED BY
CHENEY & SONS LIMITED
BANBURY, OXON

LITHOGRAPHY BY
BICESTER PHOTOLITHO LIMITED
BICESTER, ENGLAND

TYPESET IN 11/13pt TIMES ROMAN BY
HARPER PHOTOTYPESETTERS LIMITED
NORTHAMPTON, ENGLAND

© David Whitehead 1983

ISBN 0 86023 170 4

CONTENTS

INTRODUCTION & ACKNOWLEDGEMENTS

Most of the illustrations in this book date from c1850-1920. Inevitably, they provide only a partial view of the City's history and many of the great issues of the day — social reform, trade unionism, women's suffrage, the rise of the welfare state — are hardly reflected. The early photographers and illustrators of the City were not passionate social reformers. The professionals among them, like W.H. Bustin of Palace Yard, earned a livelihood from taking portraits, photographing shop fronts for advertisements and recording great events ranging from Royal visits to the local cattle show. Occasionally, they photographed an intimate scene for purely aesthetic reasons — often they seem merely to have been trying out a new piece of equipment — but rarely did they deliberately seek out a 'real life' scene, let alone the squalor and degradation of the hopeless poor. In 1900 the press had yet to realise the sensational value of a 'live' photograph. The amateur photographer was even less likely to show any social commitment. Photography was a popular but relatively expensive hobby and, after photographing the family and the house, it was the grand monuments like the Cathedral that drew the attention. He generally took for granted, much as we do to-day, the everyday occurrences of the City. The few candid photographs in this collection are all the more remarkable because of their rarity. This book therefore chronicles the changes that have occurred in the physical make-up of the City — inhabitants as well as buildings.

The population of Hereford in 1901 was 21,382. It had more than trebled since 1801 and was still rising; the mortality rate in 1893 was 20 per 1000, the birth rate 25 per 1000. Most of these people lived within the historic City and the three mid-Victorian suburbs either side of Eign Road, Whitecross and the Moorfields. The outlines of these extensions to Hereford had been established in the 1850s but, as surviving date stones indicate, they were still receiving houses in the first decades of the present century. On the hills to the north of the City, and on Broomy Hill, large houses in spacious gardens were still being built in 1900, although once again the direction of development had been established long before. The provision of piped water on the northern heights, following the erection of the water tower in 1882, was probably a decisive factor. In that year Charles Anthony, 'the founder of modern Hereford' according to William Collins, built Glenview on the summit of Eign Hill and a similar response can be detected on Aylestone Hill. Here the situation had been stabilised in mid-century, by the creation of the Penn Grove estate, which prevented further development. In 1900 there were only seven select houses in Venn's Lane, but the sale of the 44 acre estate in 1908 changed all this, and in the following year the first houses in the Garden City were erected in Bulmer Avenue.

The commercial directories indicate that the 1880s were a period of rapid growth for Hampton Park — Hafod Road — Bodenham Road. Surprisingly, many of the first inhabitants of Hereford's middle class suburbs were outsiders. By 1916 the growth of Hereford had become a political issue and a letter-writer to the *Hereford Times* complained of the 'colonies of jerry built houses growing up in the suburbs of the City'. With nearly 4,000 new houses about to be erected at Belmont before AD 2000, this plea has a topical ring. Nevertheless, in 1900 the countryside was still visible at the end of virtually every street — at the top of Old Eign Hill, above Bodenham Road, to the north of Barrs Court Road, behind the Racehorse Inn and beyond the Moorfields. Across the river, the built-up area had not changed since the 13th century, when the Royal forest of Haywood started at Drybridge House. Pool Farm, Causeway Farm and Hinton Court were still working agricultural units and St Martin's Church was an isolated monument out in the fields. When the Hinton Court estate of 204 acres was sold in 1892, the agents suggested, in rather small print, that there were numerous building sites 'unsurpassed in the neighbourhood of Hereford'. The same hope was still being entertained when the estate was sold again in 1927.

From the viewpoint of the townsman, the countryside around Hereford never looked better than it did in the two decades before the Great War. Agriculture in England had gradually surrendered to foreign competition, and wheat prices reached their lowest point for more than a century in 1894. Rents dropped, land went out of cultivation and the agricultural labourer fled to the towns. In Herefordshire these trends reinforced the pastoral character of the landscape, as farmers fought their losses by turning to grazing, which required less capital and less labour. Thus, it is easy to be lyrical about the countryside in 1900 with its scrubby fields, overgrown hedges and decaying cottages. Of course, the sale of farmland at remarkably low prices provided an opportunity for the urban middle classes — and the occasional retired farmer — to buy a large plot for his house at Holmer and Hampton Park.

This is not the place to try and assess the impact of the agricultural depression; smaller towns certainly suffered, but Hereford as a county capital and cathedral city, the service centre of the southern Marches, was cushioned from its worst effects. The coming of the railways undoubtedly encouraged economic growth, even perhaps a minor Industrial Revolution. A commercial survey of the City in 1892 shows that most of its industries, like corn factoring, cider making, brewing, tanning and wool sorting, were dependent upon the agricultural setting of the City. Brick and tile making was perhaps the only industry not specific to the locality. The railway, however, enabled these businesses, for the first time, to compete in markets beyond the immediate hinterland of the City. The Hereford Brewery sold beer in Birmingham, Godwin's tiles were world famous, Messrs Herron and Son sent their leather to Yeovil and Worcester. Yet, as the illustrations in this book show, the basic commercial unit of the City remained the family business.

In physical terms the town was not static. The Lamp Act of 1774 had inaugurated a great age of improvement, which had cleared away a good deal of the mediaeval fabric of the City — walls, gates, narrow streets and non-conforming buildings such as the Butchers Row, the Old Market Hall and even St Nicholas's Church. The Act of 1854 had brought more positive benefits — main sewers, piped water and new markets. Progress in this direction continued until the Great War. Gas was gradually connected to 4,500 houses in 1901, leaving only 65 houses in the outer liberty without this form of fuel. The City was lit by incandescent mantles in 1904. Electricity arrived in 1899 and, within two years, cables were laid as far as Wye Bridge and Aylestone Hill. The previous year, the first telephone exchange was opened in East Street. The new sewage works, proposed in 1854, was finally completed in 1890; the sewage was pumped by the Meldrum destructor in Edgar Street, which consumed 5,000 tons of the City's refuse every year. The waterworks was extended in 1911 and was capable of pumping four million gallons per year. A new slaughter house employing 'Greeners humane system' had also been recently established in Stonebow Road. Thus, the Chairman of the Society of Medical Officers, which met in Hereford in 1904, could declare 'we all knew that Hereford was a model city, a progressive place, but what has struck me particularly are the signs of continual progress'. Virtually every year in this era saw a new institutional building added to the City — the Working Boys Home, Bath Street (1880), the Dispensary, Union Street (1881), the Post Office, Broad Street (1881), the Victoria Eye and Ear Hospital (1889), the Infection Hospital, Tupsley (1893), St James's Infant School (1896), the YWCA building, St Owen Street (1902), the Town Hall (1902) — and a host of others. When, in 1911, the first Labour Exchange was erected on the corner of Gomond Street/Commercial Street, Hereford had its full complement of modern facilities and utilities.

The opening of the Victoria Eye Hospital in 1889 marked an important stage in the architectural history of the City. It was designed by E.H. Lingen-Barker, a local man, in what the newspaper described as 'a free treatment of the Queen Anne style'. Hitherto, there was little sign in Hereford that the grip of gothic and Italianate taste had slackened. Virtually all the city churches were restored or modified in this period, frequently in a manner which alarmed discriminating observers like Alfred Watkins who, as a member of the Society for the Protection of Ancient Buildings, protested via the newspaper about Oldrid Scott's work at All Saints in 1901. When the Town Hall arrived in 1902 'Queen Anne' was already the dominant style and native architects like George Godsell, who designed the Imperial, Widemarsh Street (1900) and the St Owen's Gate Dwellings (1902), were already experimenting with vernacular revivalism. The Garden City was begun in 1909, and with it the architectural tone of Hereford was decided for the next 30 years.

In 1900 Hereford was still basically a timber-framed City although, as many of these photographs show, the rustic quality of many of the buildings was hidden behind a plaster veneer. One can only regret the passing of so much excellent architecture during this period. Unfortunately, whereas in the 18th and early 19th centuries the usual practice was to build a parapet wall in front of an older shell, in 1900 'comprehensive' redevelopment tended to be the norm. But, since the architectural profession was still bound by an academic discipline committed to reviving the architecture of past ages, and was not seeking to express itself in some abstract form, even mediocre buildings contribute something of interest to the streetscape. Following in the wake of Ruskin, there was a deep concern for proper building materials. This is often reflected in the descriptions of new buildings in the newspaper, where the source of stone and brick is usually mentioned. Most materials were still local and thus, however diverse the buildings, there was always textural harmony.

The City in 1900 was also much more dense. In photograph after photograph, especially those which show the secondary streets, where once there was a building, to-day there is an open space — usually a car park. It could be argued that these were merely back-land slums, and it cannot be denied that sub-standard housing existed in Hereford then. The City Council was apparently reluctant to implement the Houses for the Working Classes Act 1890, and it took an order from the Local Government Board in 1908 to persuade it to complete the negotiations with the landlords involved, and to demolish 'the dens of Bewell Street'. Sadly, it did not implement the positive aspect of the order, which was to erect some 'garden city' dwellings, and Bewell Street became an industrial area.

Notwithstanding the 'dens of Bewell Street' and the stark statistics recorded in the reports of the Medical Officer of Health — in 1893, 119 children under five died in the City, scarlet fever resulted in 16 deaths, smallpox 12, whooping cough 8, dysentery 6 — one cannot help feeling that, in environmental terms, the City was in better heart and closer to the character to the continental cities to which English tourists flock to-day. In particular, there was a better balance between commercial and domestic life. Every photograph taken of High Town, for instance, shows curtains at first floor windows. Historic buildings in 1900 were still serving the purpose for which they had been created; the separation of home and trade was still unusual in the centre of the City, and master and journeyman still lived at either end of the same alley.

Most people in 1900 sought their recreation within the compass of the City. Hereford throbbed with clubs and societies, which filled seven sides of Jakeman and Carver's *Directory* in 1902. Many of them functioned within the 111 licensed premises which at this date were under attack by the temperance movement. The Chief Constable of Hereford, Frank Richardson, responding to some statements made at a meeting of the Church of England Temperance Society, claimed that the City was essentially a sober community, with only 186 cases of drunkenness in 1894, 91 of which were offences by non-residents, especially hop-pickers, and miners tramping from South Wales to the Midland coalfield. (Chesterfield, with 73 pubs, had 312 cases.) Sobriety, on this evidence, was yet another of the benefits Hereford enjoyed, because it had missed the Industrial Revolution.

As a result perhaps of the social homogeneity of Hereford, private charity was still a feature of *fin de siecle* society. Although, in 1906 the Liberal government began laying the foundations of the welfare state, the first response of the better-off citizens of Hereford in the face of a disaster such as severe weather conditions, was to set up a relief committee. The first two weeks of February 1895 were cold and, within a matter of days, funds were being raised by the Mayor to purchase coal. The weather quickly improved, but 61 tons of fuel had been distributed to those who required it. Although, of course, the poor should not have been poor, the speed with which the community reacted and the motives of the relief committee cannot be faulted. In a City where all but a few of the suburban dwellers lived cheek by jowl, the atrocious exploitation of the poor, which was a feature of large industrial cities, caused in part by the physical separation of the rich and poor, was unlikely to occur. Not only did the fabric of Hereford remain relatively unscathed in 1900, but the social structure which had nurtured its character also survived. The era depicted in these photographs was not a Golden Age, but what a pity, with all the advantages of life in 1982, that a little more of 'old Hereford' did not survive.

My thanks are due, first and foremost, to the many illustrators of Hereford whose water colours, engravings and photographs have found their way into the collections at the Hereford City Library and the County Record Office. This book belongs to them.

In many cases an attribution is made in the text but special mention ought to be made of the photographs taken by Alfred Watkins and F.C. Morgan collected in the City Library. For allowing me to make use of these, I should like to thank Mr B.L. Whitehouse, the City Librarian, and Robin Hill, whose comprehensive knowledge of the contents of the Reference Library helped to provide the historical context for many of the illustrations.

With the kind permission of Mr P. Dean and Mr K. Jones I was able to skim the surface of the vast collection of negatives taken by W.H. Bustin in the Hereford Record Office, where I was aided by Miss Sue Hubbard and other members of the Record Office staff. Mr Percy Pritchard kindly placed his collection of photographs at my disposal, while Nigel Heins provided a photograph of his great great grandfather.

Finally, since the originals for all the illustrations in this book are still in their respective collections, I obviously owe a great deal to my father Anthony Whitehead, who employed the skills and artistry of the modern photographer in providing all the prints for the illustrations.

HEREFORD WITHOUT

ABOVE LEFT

Around most cities c1900 there was still an unchanging rural world with roots stretching back to a time before cities. So it is here at Lugwardine. This world, which was to be shattered by mass communications, was captured in water colour by artists such as David Cox and Helen Allingham, and in music by Bax, Butterworth and, slightly later, Vaughan Williams. Many of these images of the past are blatantly nostalgic and this photograph is riddled with self-consciousness, but the props are authentic and the setting exquisite. All this has gone. There was poetry in old England, which nourished the spirit, and in surroundings like this must have kept at bay the damp and sudden death.

BELOW

Such was the view from the Vineyard, Hampton Bishop Road c1890. The Bodenhams were still lords of Rotherwas, and this was their wheat harvest ripening in stooks on the alluvial flood plain of the Wye. Soon these fields were to sprout Nissen huts and bunkers, which produced a rather different crop for export to Flanders. Above the fields, Rotherwas Park Wood stretches like a deciduous rug along the ridge. As a private game reserve, it was not threatened by felling orders and cash-crop forestry, like its successor. This view stimulated the creativity of Sir Edward Elgar, who would have risen to this prospect from the bedroom windows of Plas Gwyn. In the foreground is the thatched boathouse of Vineyard Croft — the ultimate picturesque conceit.

ABOVE RIGHT

Domesday Book records that, in the time of Edward the Confessor, every burgage holder in Hereford had to spend one day every year gathering hay wherever the sheriff pleased. Here in the Lugg Meadows on a hazy afternoon in June, in the reign of another Edward, their successors carried out the same task. Two bonnetted matrons, well protected against the insects and the sun, turn the hay, while their companions raise the sweet-smelling crop, enriched with the wilted stems of hayrattle and knapweed, onto a horsedrawn waggon. Francis Kilvert enjoyed a similar occasion in 1875 when, on Midsummer's Day, 'over the thick waving fragrant grass came the sweet country music of the white-sleeved mowers wheting their scythes and the voices of their children at play among the fresh-cut flowery swathes'. Today, the women with their dark skirts and high collared blouses seem over-dressed. But this was peasant's work and not lady's play.

This picturesque cottage in Baynton Wood, overlooking the Lugg meadows at Tupsley, was the home of David Cox between 1815-17. Cox, who was one of the most lyrical interpreters of the English landscape in the early 19th century, came to Hereford as a drawing master at Miss Coucher's school in Widemarsh Street, to escape the dispiriting effects of the Industrial Revolution, and to seek inspiration from the border countryside. This house, George Cottage in Cox's time, with its rough rendered walls, rustic porch, deep thatch and lattice windows epitomises the wayside cots of the humble labourer which figure frequently in Cox's paintings. From here the artist could enjoy a variety of pastoral landscapes: the meadows purple with knapweed in June, haymaking, the winter floods and the shadowy backwaters of the Lugg Rhea with its decrepit willows. Sadly, the cottage was burnt down in 1923, most of the trees have been felled and the prospect marred by electricity pylons and modern housing.

BELOW

David Cox's cottage in leafy Venn's Lane. Cox moved in 1817 to a purpose-built cottage-cum-studio in Parry's Lane. His landlord, Mr Parry, 'who held a sympathetic opinion of artists' gave £40 towards the building; Cox provided a further £30. The garden was planted with hollyhocks, Cox's favourite flowers and already, it seems, a symbol of vernacular charm. There was a well in the garden in which Mrs Cox used to hang her meat, until it was stolen just before she was due to receive some guests for dinner. In 1823 Cox moved across the road and built a fine gothick house, then called Ash Tree House and to-day known as Little Abbey.

LEFT AND BELOW

In 1925, to improve the flow of water, the Lugg Drainage Board demolished the weir and a major part of the Lugg Mills. Until the 1880s the mill had two wheels, driving seven pairs of stones, which ground flour for several Hereford bakers. Although the timber-framed structure suspended across the river looks older, most of the buildings were erected c1810 by Richard Price, who also constructed a coal wharf — shown in the foreground — where Forest of Dean coal was unloaded from barges and was for sale, according to the *Hereford Journal*, 'at same price as at Hereford'. Earlier, the mill had been used for fulling in connection with the City's cloth trade, for a presentment of 1569 refers to 'iii styckes & an hâlfe of wyte wollen cloth' stolen from here. In the Middle Ages the mill belonged to the Bishop of Hereford as an appurtenance of the manor of Nether Shelwick, and in 1404 was described as 'a fulling mill of no yearly value because wasted for many years past'. The mill stones were apparently given to the Hereford Museum.

RIGHT

A pair of recently pollarded elms shade the intimate forecourt of the Whalebone Inn at the bottom of Old Eign Hill. The tap room of this modest Georgian building once throbbed with the voices of bowhauliers, steersmen and wharfingers, for across the road — not the Hampton Bishop Road which was only formally adopted in 1891 — a narrow path led down to Eign Wharf on the Wye. Here coal and timber were landed close to a dam constructed in the late 17th century, to provide a deep-water passage for trows navigating the shallows below the Vineyard. The boatmen who came here brought the whale bones which once provided an unusual entrance to the pub. With the collapse of the navigation in 1855, the Whalebone slumbered until 1956, when the license was transferred to an adjoining house — now the Salmon. Lacking its first floor, the truncated remains of the old pub serve to-day as a veterinary surgery.

Alfred Watkins was a founder member of the Herefordshire Beekeepers' Association and, until 1901, its honorary secretary. During the 1890s, from the vantage point of the Hereford Brewery dray, he scoured the countryside for signs of beekeeping, producing a set of original photographs demonstrating various aspects of bee culture. Here, Mr Turner of New Rents, Lugwardline stoops to pick strawberries in the shadow of his picturesque cottage, near an osier-thatched skep. By the First World War, after a series of epidemics, the frame hive became ubiquitous. No more were these buzzing fertility symbols seen in the cottage gardens of Herefordshire.

A lyrical painting by James Wathen of Eign Mill, now an industrial estate adjoining Foley Street. The 'molendinum de Yghen' — from the Welsh word *iain* meaning 'cold' — is referred to in the early 13th century, along with 'scuttemulin' on the Ledbury Road, as a possession of the Dean and Chapter of Hereford. A wealthy citizen called William the Goldsmith held it at the substantial rent of 50s per annum. He presumably recovered this payment from the tenants of the Dean and Chapter, who had to take their grain to this mill and, as part of the feudal services, also had to periodically clean the mill-pond and, when required, carry new stones to the mill. On an early 19th century map, the mill-pond is shown stretching up the Eign Brook towards the Ledbury Road. By this date the mill belonged to the City Council and was occupied by Issac Jones who, rather conveniently, also possessed Scutt Mill.

Hereford framed in elms from the fields near Barrs Court in 1795 — long before the canal and the railway turned this area into the entrepôt of the City. Widemarsh Street, with the Essex Arms and the Coningsby Hospital, can perhaps be seen on the right. The sketch was made by James Wathen (1751-1828), the Hereford glover-turned-globe-trotter, and friend of Byron, who contributed many drawings of Herefordshire antiquities to the *Gentleman's Magazine* and other topographical publications.

The same piece of Hereford half a century later, after the arrival of the Hereford and Gloucester Canal in 1845: the print shows one of the three arms of the Hereford basin, with Edward George's timber yard on the right. Although the print exaggerates the commercial activity on the canal, the 1850s were fairly prosperous years, partly because of the traffic in construction materials for the railway. *Lascelles Directory* for 1851 mentions four carriers operating from the wharf, and there was a daily service between Hereford and Gloucester. Like most industrial innovations in the 19th century, the basin was an object of curiosity and, fed by the pure waters of the Eign Brook, the fishing was also good.

Before the First World War, Hereford was embraced on the west by 'gentry' landscapes. The well wooded park of the Bodenhams at Rotherwas ran along the ridge of Dinedor and was only divided from the estate of Francis Richard Wegg-Prosser — sometime lord of the Royal forest of Haywood — by Ridge Hill and the Callow. This photograph shows the house at Belmont, designed by A.W. Pugin in the Early English style c1860, which totally transformed an earlier house, built by Col John Mathews MP in 1788. This mansion, built of smooth Bath stone with a rounded bay and Georgian windows, was designed by James Wyatt — also architect of Sufton Court, Mordiford. It can be seen on the frontage overlooking the Wye. Mathews also employed the landscape architect Humphrey Repton, but the great Atlas Cedar in the foreground must be part of the Victorian planting. C1900 the house was let to Philip F. Walker, FRGS, FRHS who is presumably one of those pictured here.

A mid-19th century view of Belmont from Breinton Springs before the house was altered in the 1860s. One of the 'great ornaments' of the Wye, according to that discriminating tourist, Rev W. Gilpin, was its woods. Yet Gilpin also noted that the chief deficiency of the valley was the lack of 'large trees on the edge of the water; which clumped here and there, would diversify the hills as the eye passes them, and remove the heaviness which always, in some degree arises from the continuity of ground'. Here at Belmont Dr Mathews, aided by Repton, rectified this defect, turning a steep sheep pasture into the epitome of a 'picturesque landscape'. In 1756 John Price could write 'Nature seems to have been in a high degree favourable to this spot, and where she was found deficient, art conducted by the truest taste, has succeeded in the attempt to embellish it . . .'. And so it was when Dr Mathews died in 1826. The *Hereford Journal* observed that 'the scenery of our highly favoured county has borrowed additional charms from his tasteful hands'. Unfortunately, Dutch elm disease and recent felling have removed the clumped trees in the foreground and reduced the 'artful diversity' of the scene.

James Wathen's water colour of Belmont in 1822 with a certain amount of nakedness still apparent as Dr Mathew's planting gradually envelops the house.

'Not everyone can live at Rotherwas' was the response in the late 17th century by the local antiquarian Blount to the breathtaking location of the family seat of the Bodenhams. Squeezed between Dinedor Hill and the Wye, few country houses had within so small a compass such varied scenery, and all within the sound of the cathedral bells. To-day, in order to grasp the sublime qualities of the site, one must remove an armaments factory, a sewage works and an industrial estate. This photograph, looking south towards Dinedor, shows the house built by Charles Bodenham in 1732 to the designs of James Gibbs. The herbalist Gerard recorded in 1597: 'I have seen in the pastures about the grounds of a worshipful gentleman's dwell-house, about 2 miles from Hereford, Roger Bodenham Esq., so many apple trees of all sorts that the servants drank for the most part no other drinke but that which is made of apples'. The tree in the foreground appears to be a pear, while to the right is a Spanish chestnut. The park was once the happy hunting ground of the Woolhope Naturalists Field Club, who regularly came with tape measures to register the passing of time by surveying the great trees. Some of the old magic of Rotherwas can still be experienced beyond the grassy platform which supported the house, where a formal walk passes around the mellow brick wall of the kitchen garden. Along a cow-trod path, box hedges grow in profusion, untouched since 1913, when the last estate gardener packed away his shears. On warm days, the exotic oils released from the hedge remind one of the Renaissance gardens of Southern Europe. At the end of the walk, beneath a walnut tree, a few scattered stones mark the site of a private quay, where coal was unloaded from Wye trows to fuel the great house. On summer evenings, sand martins fill the air above the river — as no doubt they did when Blount knew the house in its hey-day.

These precious chimney pieces were removed from Rotherwas in 1913 and sent to the United States, 'Much to the great regret of those interested in the country's art treasures' commented the *Country Life*. With the exception perhaps of the mutilated overmantle at Canon Frome, nothing like the left-hand piece survives in the county to-day. With its allegorical figures, carved in the round, and achievement of twenty-five coats, it represents the first flush of the Renaissance in Herefordshire and must date from c1580. The other piece, albeit equally monumental, is rather mannered, and in character conventionally Jacobean. They originally, stood in 'the noble Dyning Room' and 'fair Parlour' of Sir Roger Bodenham's house 'new built of stone' and were subsequently re-erected in Charles Bodenham's house of 1732.

Below the Callow on a winter day in 1928, the high road out of Hereford still has a rough earthy texture, easily creased by the narrow wheels of the early motor vehicles, some of which can be seen parked in the courtyard of the Angel Inn. In these quieter, less hurried days, the weary lorry driver presumably saw nothing untoward in stopping for a few pints. The pub is still there, but now a private house, while the road, kerbed and white lined, has lost its hedge and is almost three times as wide. The many-transomed telegraph poles — a familiar scene on all main roads a few years ago — have also gone, so perhaps there has been some environmental improvement.

Until the 1930s, Hereford, in physical terms, ended to the west at St Martin's. The road to Ross forked left at Drybridge, past a row of timber-framed cottages — now the traffic island — with the St Martin's National School opposite, where the Welsh Club stands to-day. In the 19th century the turnpike road to Ross left Hereford at Hinton Lane and went via Putson, Rotherwas, Holme Lacy and Hoarwithy. The present Ross Road was basically the way to Monmouth. Just round the corner, Hinton Farm and Court stood amid extensive orchards, overlooking the flood plain of the Wye. From the earliest times, the property had belonged to the Cathedral, hence the Old English *higna-tun* = 'the monks town'. In the 12th century it became a prebendal estate. The engraving reproduced here comes from a sale catalogue of 1892, at which time the 'reputed manor' of Hinton had an estate of 204 acres, including six cottages. One of these, Hinton Cottage, which still stands opposite the Ship Inn, was described as a 'gentleman's residence'. The 'commodious' Court 'situated in park-like lands' surrounded by small fields edged with pollarded elms was, from the evidence of the print, an elegant early Georgian house. A photograph of 1931, however, shows a timber-framed range with a gabled porch, and suggests greater antiquity, which was confirmed by a window in the hall containing fragments of mediaeval glass. During the 16th and 17th centuries, Hinton belonged to a branch of the Clements family of Putson. In 1892 the rural environment of Hinton was already threatened for, in the words of the catalogue, 'building sites are numerous and unsurpassed in the neighbourhood of Hereford'.

LEFT

Holmer Hall, the home of J. Orr-Ewing Esq, set in its 8 acres of mature grounds, including an ornamental fishpond, for sale in 1901, and already the development potential of the land was being explored. City gas was laid to the gates, and the adjoining road frontages 'present most picturesque building sites'. Remarkably, it was not until the 1960s that a dormitory suburb was created. The process was completed in 1982.

BELOW

An arboretum in the making — a view from The Belvedere, Broomy Hill c1900. The road from Barton can be seen beyond the stepped wall on the left; Broomy Hill Farm in the Gorewell is in the middle distance below the railway embankment, and through the bank of trees surrounding the playing field beneath the Antelope pub, one arch of Wye Bridge can be seen. Here the garden of Mrs R.S. Paterson was planted with exotic conifers, including a monkey puzzle. It was this sort of judicious, long-term planting which gave Broomy Hill its special bosky quality, which survives to-day. Although in this case the garden was soon to be sub-divided for building plots, the cedars, holm oaks, cypresses and firs planted in neighbouring gardens at about the same date are still with us to-day.

RIGHT

According to a sale catalogue produced when the 'Belvidere' was sold in 1912 'the abundant water supply and sanitary arrangements' of Broomy Hill contributed to the low death rate of this part of the City. The house had two WCs and a pump for spring water. Corporation gas was connected, but the electric light cable passed by in the street — Mrs Paterson, it seems, could live without such novelties.

In 1909 Mrs E.F. Bulmer opened the first houses built by the Hereford Co-operative Housing Ltd on the lower slopes of Aylestone Hill. Within three years 85 cottages had been erected, and a new era of humanitarian architecture had dawned for Hereford. The 'garden city' movement, which had begun in Letchworth and Hampstead in 1905-06, had arrived in Hereford in 1908 and, during the next two decades, idealised suburbs sprouted in the Portfields and moved forward up the hill towards the Training College. These vernacular cottages, directly inspired by the Arts and Crafts movement, set in spacious gardens along tree-lined streets, represent the climax of municipal housing in Hereford. The architects were Groome and Bettington, later joined by R.A. Ford. As these drawings indicate, they had fully absorbed the novel vocabulary of C.F.A. Voysey — generous steeply pitched roofs, high gables, rough-cast walls and bands of mullion windows. Sadly, the final designs accepted by the Housing Company were rather less adventurous but even to-day the 'cottages' of Bulmer and Lingen Avenues mix easily with the Tudoresque houses of Penn Grove Road.

END ELEVATION

YESTERDAY'S TOWN

ABOVE

High Town in 1902 and no sign of an automobile: the dung on the road is still fresh, ready to be scraped up by the City scavenger and sold to the farmers beyond the suburbs. An emancipated woman, perhaps from Hampton Park, in a spacious blouse, cautiously 'cycles past. Two policemen with white helmets pad along the pavement *en route* to their beats, after signing in at the station in Gaol Street. They walk together for conviviality, not protection. The Midland Carrier pauses after hauling a heavy load from his cart, unhindered by yellow lines and confident that there is plenty of room for other vehicles. How difficult it is to realise that, notwithstanding creaking carts and clicking horses' hooves, the dominant sound in those car-less days came from people and not their machines.

BELOW

High Town in 1905: across the world the Japanese have just sunk the Russian Imperial Navy with a secret weapon called the Whitehead torpedo. The workers are on the streets in Petrograd, but in Hereford the Market Hall clock strikes a quarter past five, and tea is still being served for weary shoppers from Dorstone and Dinedor in the City and County Dining Rooms. The cabbies wait for their fares, chatting and lounging beside their vehicles, much as they do to-day. Their hut now stands in the Bishop's Meadow. Pedestrians and 'cyclists cross the street with complete informality, horse-drawn vehicles are pulled up in front of the shops, where it is most convenient. Mr Wilson, the photographer, receives scant attention except from the delivery boy. Lloyds Bank occupies the recently restored Old House. A customer has parked his car against the railings.

Could any book about Hereford possibly ignore that much photographed antiquity — the Old House? Finally isolated in 1837, it passed through a variety of hands before being purchased by the Worcester Bank in 1883. This company thoroughly restored the building, adding most of the windows on the ground floor and on the east and west ends. In 1928 Lloyds Bank made a gift of the property to the City Council. In 1860 the Old House was occupied by John Roberts, saddler and harness maker. The framing at the west end — a credit to the carpenter's craft — before 1837 would have been a partition wall. The shop front was added c1820, when the chimney was also crenellated, suggesting the house was already regarded as a gothick curiosity.

LEFT

In 1874 there are few changes. Mr Smith was also a saddler but more reticent about displaying his wares. The exposed framing on the west end is about to disappear.

RIGHT

Three years later the framing has gone, and Mathew Oatfield, ironmonger and earthenware dealer, is well and truly in occupation. The last authentic 17th century window on the ground floor has been replaced by a new pentice and counter for Henry Fletcher, fishmonger.

ABOVE

A great deal has changed at this end of High Town since c1910. Brigg's were soon to occupy the corner site, where the New Co-operative Store stood at the time of this photograph. Marchant's was absorbed when the bank was rebuilt in the 1930s. The London City and Midland Bank was a recent arrival in 1910 and was perhaps the *raison d'etre* of the photograph. Round in High Street, beneath the fine gabled Italianate building, there was Nurse and Co, fishmongers, and next door, Hepworths. Both these excellent buildings — perhaps less than 50 years old — were swept away in 1928 for the Marks and Spencers Bazaar, which still stands and must have been Hereford's first example of 'modern' architecture. When the modest late Georgian facades beyond were replaced in 1932, the short-lived timber-framed revival was in full swing.

LEFT

These splendid Neo-classical facades, dripping with stucco ornament, can still be seen in High Town to-day, but without their ground floors. When the premises were sold in 1913 on the retirement of Mr William Pearce, grocer, who had traded for 'upwards of half a century', they symbolised an economic/residential unit as old as the town itself. Something similar had occupied the same site from the mid-11th century when High Town was first laid out as an extension to Anglo-Saxon Hereford. Mr Pearce lived above and behind his shop in a well appointed four-bedroomed house with 'hot water pipes', marble fireplaces and gas lighting. All around him were the supporting spaces of his trade; wine and spirit vaults, offices, counting house, warehouses and even a cottage fronting East Street, perhaps occupied by an employee. Across the narrow passage which serviced the premises was his neighbour and tenant, Albert Townsend, optician, who occupied a similar but more compact shop-cum-house. The whole plot (170' × 42') still occupied a single burgage laid out 850 years before, across the decaying pre-Conquest defences of the City.

RIGHT

Eign Street c1890: one of those rare photographs which capture an age in a single frame. It's a dull morning; the mist mixes with the smoke of innumerable coal fires and obscures the view of the far end of the street where the Red Lion stands. The road sweepers have just passed this way, their brushes graining the animal deposit which covers the gutter and gives a sticky texture to the road. The sulphurous atmosphere has all but eroded the 15th century mouldings on the porch of All Saints church. The fading tracks leading to the church suggest there had been a service earlier. The iron gates, bent by climbing boys, are now closed. The street scene is enlivened with hanging lamps, pawn brokers' balls and a miscellany of unregulated signs.

Eign Street c1900 displayed a remarkable range of shops — and an exhibition of youthful vulgarity. Here were bootmakers, pawnbrokers, tobacconists, butchers, game merchants, cabinetmakers, saddlers, drapers, fishmongers, carpenters, seedsmen, hairdressers, newsagents, hatters and, of course, several pubs — the Greyhound, Barrell, Maidenhead and Three Crowns. To-day a majority of the services and goods can be provided by a single shop such as Woolworths. The pattern of building on the north side of the street has changed little, but the south side has fared less well, partly because of the City Council's misdirected scheme — maintained between c1930-70 — of widening the street for through traffic.

Hereford's principal thoroughfare, *fin de siecle* Broad Street on a quiet weekday morning. On both sides of the street the accretions of the Victorian age — the Library, the Catholic Church, the Corn Exchange, the Post Office, the Green Dragon — have produced a monumental scene. How superbly All Saints Church closes the view.

Offa Street 'is obviously ancient because two vehicles cannot pass each other' declared Alfred Watkins, who proceeded to demonstrate how the alignment of a pond on Aylestone Hill, St Peter's Church, the Cathedral and a prominent group of trees at Haywood placed Offa Street at the hub of a 'ley line'. To-day, with the demolition of all the buildings on the left, the street looks less ancient and is no longer a 'promising ancient trackway'. Until 1858, Offa Street was known as Little Milk Lane — after the dairy of the canons which stood on the site of Harley House — and earlier, in the 14th century, simply as the 'Aley'. Like Church Street and Barroll Lane, it started life as a narrow passage through the earliest defences of the city, connecting the Anglo-Saxon 'low town' with the Norman High Town.

Here's a puzzle for those who only know to-day's City. Whitefriars Street no longer exists, except as an anonymous road junction in front of St Nicholas' Church. But in c1910, King Street, St Nicholas Street and Whitefriars Street ran into Barton Road, with an unbroken building line on the south side. The buildings on the left here stand in the Greyfriars carpark; the gates belong to the Red House, opening to-day onto Greyfriars Avenue, then an unadopted lane, which led to the Barton Bathing Station — the chalet seen in the distance. The house on the right was one of a group of 13 cottages which formed an island in the middle of the road called Inner Friars. The first building on the left, with brick string courses and segmental headed windows flush with the brickwork, is early Georgian — a terraced version of Bewell House. But for a 'ley line' identified by Alfred Watkins running from All Saints Church to Merry Hill Coppice in the distance, this corner of Hereford would have fallen unrecorded.

The scene from the rear window of the Town Hall in 1922 — in many respects, a pretty, but unremarkable, view of the Cathedral and Harley Court. But on closer inspection it seems the Town Hall had fine cast iron gates to East Street, each enriched with a central cartouche and flanked by brick and terracotta columns with ball finials — the natural complement to the Town Hall. What ever happened to these elegant objects? Nearby, the old stable block, which disappeared in 1974, is dressed in Virginia creeper, and around it are the vestiges of Richard Johnson's garden.

Deep in the town ditch, beneath an ivy-covered bastion, Grey Friars House looked out in 1900 across a pleasant garden whence, on warm summer days, the bees swarmed towards the clover in the Barton meadows. The house took its name from the monastery of the Franciscan Friars, established in this suitably humbling environment, c1228. In this oozy spot, a place as renowned for scholarship as Oxford could easily have developed. But to-day only a handful of books from the library of the Hereford Greyfriars survive. Where the water from the ditch entered the Wye, the Friars had a watermill — later in the 18th century to become a woollen manufactory, on the site of the present restaurant. The ditch was drained after the Civil War and, in a survey of 1672, it was occupied as a garden by Herbert Aubrey, a branch of the famous Clehonger family, who had a mansion in the remains of the conventual buildings. The late Georgian house in the photograph was occupied in 1900 by Thomas Theophilus Davies JP, but to-day it is besieged by the Ring Road, and its neighbours in St Nicholas Street (which does not occur on the modern town map) have been demolished.

A view across the river towards St Martin's, just above Wye Bridge, in 1870. The essence of Hereford's vernacular tradition is distilled in the group of venerable buildings in the foreground.

The monastery of the Grey Friars stood within an enclosed precinct just below St Nicholas's Church, while the building here, known throughout the 19th century as The Friars, occupied the site of a water mill referred to at the time of the Dissolution in 1536. On Taylor's plan of the City in 1757 the site is empty, but on a view dated 1775 a thatched building is shown, which could well be a mill, adjoining a rather ramshackle quay. On Curley's plan of 1858 a millpond filled by a small stream, which ran from the Barton, is shown upstream of a substantial court-yard building — presumably part of the one shown here. This house, according to an advertisement in 1915, has 'considerable architectural attractiveness designed to blend with the picturesque beauty of the surrounding scenery'. The great wall, part-dam and part-quay, remains.

Bridge Street in the late Spring, quiet since everyone has perhaps gone to the Wesleyan chapel to hear Rev J. Meredith, the preacher proclaimed on the hoarding. The stuccoed facade of Rogers & Co, slightly projecting beyond the ground floor, hints at disguised timber framing, but the Royal Commissioners did not find any in 1931. The Crystal Room replaced these buildings.

Eign Road in 1924, not greatly changed today. The major change is the absence of St Giles' Chapel, moved to its present site facing St Owen Street during road widening in 1927.

CITY AT WORK

ABOVE

Hereford Cathedral in 1885 provided free publicity for William Stephens, painter, plumber and glazier of Gwynne Street. Stephens was also among the last to own the right to net salmon in the Wye at Hereford; hence the structure on stilts at the end of his yard, used for drying nets. The wheel-like contrivance overhanging the river was probably used to pull in the nets, which were stretched across the Wye at this point. Stephens was convinced that the shallows here marked the 'army ford' from which Hereford took its name, and so called his new house on the opposite bank, 'Ye Olde Forde'.

BELOW

Evans Cider Works on Widemarsh Common stood close to the early Georgian mansion, Moor House, just a stone's throw from the city. The proximity reflected the proprietorship of Mr William Chave who, in the late 19th century, owned both. Chave's interest in scientific knowledge, especially chemistry, demonstrated to-day by his name on a Broad Street shop, made Evans' cider one of Hereford's most famous products. At several agricultural shows in the 1880s it carried off first prize against competition from the whole of southern England. As if to challenge the south-western cider makers, one of Evans' products was called 'Devonshire'. But 'Golden Pippin', 'Barland' and 'Oldfield' were equally celebrated. The secret of success seems to have been what the Victorians called 'hygiene', and the understanding that metal and apple juice do not mix; hence the use of glazed porcelain tanks and 'india-rubber tubes'. The print shows a range of superb rustic buildings with pantiled roofs. Much mutilated, they remained until 1975. Now the site is a car park but, below the ground, like a lost catacomb, there are immense cellars capable of holding 2,000 'pipes', each with a capacity of 105 gallons.

49

Godwin's tiles were initially manufactured at Lugwardine, but the success of the business 'in the front rank of the industries of this country' encouraged the company in 1884 to construct a large factory, beside the disused Hereford and Gloucester canal in College Road, 'ensconced in a hollow surrounded on all sides by scenery of the most charming description'. A vast range of enamelled and embossed tiles was produced at the works, including 'faithful represent-ations of the whole British Flora' — wonderful collectors' items to-day. Many were destined for the fireplaces 'of the well appointed houses of the Kingdom, the Colonies and America'. Others still enrich fairly ordinary houses in the suburbs of Hereford. The company also specialised in hand-made antique tiles, some of which found their way to Windsor Castle — hence, perhaps, the name *Victoria* Tile Works.

The Old Red Sandstone clays of Holmer 'being situated close to the joint lines of the Great Western and North Western Railway' were used for brickmaking at least 40 years before Godwin's moved to College Road. Indeed, the Albert Steam Pipe, Tile, Pottery, Building and Artistic Brick Company claimed that their tiles were 'adopted exclusively by Messrs. Godwin and Hewitt' for their new works — a subtle piece of oneupmanship. In both name and products, the Albert works complemented their neighbour, specialising in facing bricks which had apparently 'successfully stood the tests applied by various architects' and were employed in lining the Dinmore Tunnel. Their ornamental bricks were used to great effect at Barrs Court Station and the County College (The Royal National College for the Blind). Goodrich Court and Thinghill Court, two of the greatest gothic houses of Herefordshire, were also partly constructed of Albert bricks. They produced 'art pottery' such as garden vases, pedestals, brackets and 'rustic stumps' all in terra cotta. The print shows the company's eight horse power, patent compound traction engine, which it had been 'compelled to purchase at great cost' in 1890.

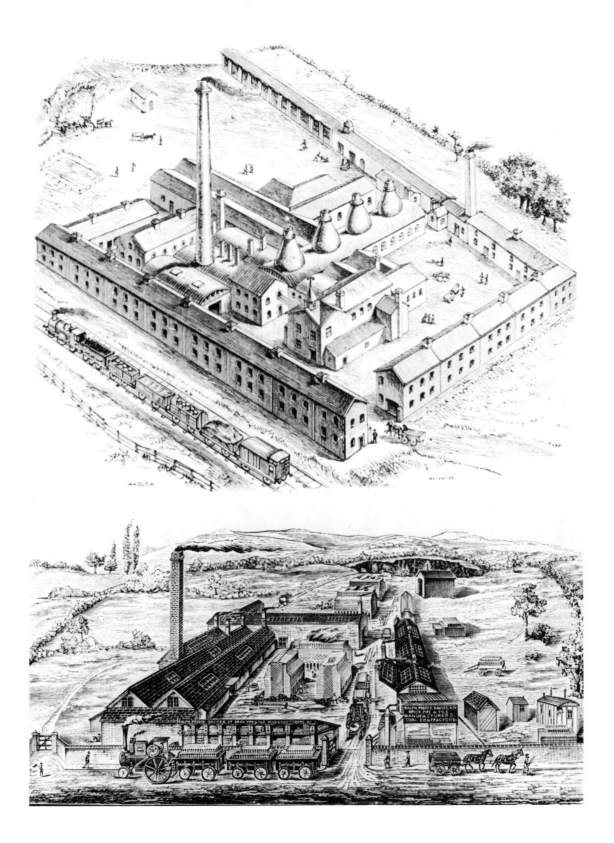

These buildings, perhaps the most pleasing commercial ensemble in Widemarsh Street Without, still survive amid a 20th century junk landscape of garages and warehouses. The range of blank arches — purpose unknown — are especially memorable as a Victorian embellishment. Ralph and Preece were colliery and brickwork proprietors for whom Davies acted as agent and carrier. He had several 'pantechnicon vans of the newest type fitted with India rubber springs' which were constructed so that they could be 'taken over the entire system of railways throughout the United Kingdom'. In an advertisement of 1892 Davies printed a number of testimonials from satisfied gentry customers. The Hon Sir Watkins Williams of Ruthin in North Wales expressed complete satisfaction with the manner in which his 'Moorish pottery' had been carried while W. Henderson Esq, of Ashford Court near Ludlow received his seventeen vans of 'wine, pictures and marble . . . rapidly and without damage'. Mr Davies modestly admitted to several hundred similar 'unsolicited' testimonials.

Hereford has always been a cornfactoring centre, distributing grain grown in the lowlands of England throughout the hill country to the west. Rogers and Co, founded in 1863, continued this tradition from their premises in Bridge Street, occupied to-day by the Crystal Room. The photograph, taken in 1890, shows a labour-intensive scene with only one piece of machinery in sight — a hand truck. The heavily laden waggon was probably one of the largest then seen in Bridge Street. Framed in the door, in bowler hat and apron, is the shop manager who, from the evidence of the curtains, lived above the shop.

Behind Bridge Street the company owned extensive warehousing, including the Alhambra Theatre. The most recent addition in 1890 was a five storey polychrome store capable of holding 8,000 bushels of grain. It is still the finest piece of industrial architecture in central Hereford. Meal was stored here, which the company claimed was consumed by 'Hereford cattle while on the voyage to the Antipodes and other parts of the world'. English agriculture was already hooked on imported fertilizers — 'artificial manures' as the sign calls them — and Rogers and Co stored a wide variety, including guano. The manager of the Commercial Road branch was then Mr George Barnes, while the agent in Ross was Mr Franklin. By the early 20th century, Rogers and Co had become Franklin Barnes, who are still with us.

CENTRE

The Alhambra was, perhaps, Hereford's least well known theatrical establishment. Entered from Gwynne Street, it was originally built as an annexe to the Royal Oak Inn in Bridge Street in the 1830s. But in 1892 it had long been 'forsaken by drama and given up to Commerce'. It continued as a seed store until demolished by Franklin Barnes and Co in 1936. This photograph by Walter Pritchard on the eve of demolition shows that it was still absolutely complete, with cast iron stanchions, gallery, raked balcony seats and gas lights.

LEFT

In 1902 Norton and Son 'private hatters, hosiers, shirt and collar makers' stood next to Chave and Jackson in Broad Street. Flannel suits and 'Grade 1 cycle stockings' also formed part of their stock-in-trade. The two great gas lamps are the most striking feature here; their bulbous character complements the baroque consoles of the shop front and the immense range of round hats. Soon after the First World War Norton's had left Hereford.

RIGHT

With alarming stubbornness, Frank Hodges, hatter, hosier and gentleman's outfitter, occupied premises either in Commercial Street or Commercial Road between c1910 and 1925 and never, as here, in St Owen Street. Although men's fashions tend to be rather static there are a few clues to help date the photograph. The trouser press was apparently invented in the 1890s but, from the evidence of Mr Hodges' 'breeches', it was still unknown in Hereford. After the Great War trousers tended to be wider and had turnups. Similarly, the continuous round collar and cravat worn by the assistant was a pre-War fashion. The incandescent gas mantle was introduced into Hereford in 1901. So, perhaps, the date is around 1910.

Butchers are a dwindling race in the modern city. There were 35 operating from the principal streets of Hereford in 1851; to-day there are only 12. These two photographs were probably taken at Christmas. Mr Aston, we are told, had 'twelve yards of frontage on a leading thoroughfare' with 'spotless marble slabs, bright clean cutlery, handsome fittings and a splendid show of meat . . . one of the sights of Eign Street'. Mr Constable's premises in Widemarsh Street — opposite the Black Swan — were a little more primitive. The tone of the photograph is set by the stained aprons of the proprietor and his assistants but matters are not improved by the sticky litter in the gutter. The horned heads and array of gutted carcases with bowels protruding are almost an incitement to vegetarianism. The subscribers to Constable's meat club are certainly welcome to THIS OX which is apparently about to engulf the lad on the right. Equally, the effectiveness of the invitation PLEASE WALK IN is somewhat diminished by Mr Constable's menacing pose. His sombre expression and dark form help to explain why, in the past, butchers were often the first suspects examined in the wake of a murder.

RIGHT

Now an irrelevance, this fine piece of Jacobean timber-framing, with its elaborate Marcher enrichments, was once stuffed with oriental teas, pickles, jams, jellies, bon bons, cosaques, Lazenby's soups, Armour's Paysandu tinned tongues and 1,001 epicurean delights. It seems only yesterday that the aroma of freshly ground coffee drifted from the ventilators up over the treacly facade. In the Edwardian era, Marchant and Mathews prided themselves on their 'old fashioned respectability' and could claim a pedigree as local traders back to the 1770s. They were also conscious of the architectural charms of their premises, 'which never fails to attract the admiration of visitors and of all those who feel an interest in the survival of the characteristic features of picturesque Old Hereford'. To-day the fragment which remains is a monument to the false values of the 1960s.

According to a commercial eulogy written in the late 19th century, Hereford's reputation as an 'advanced musical centre' was in part derived from the 'presence in the city of a permanent musical depot' belonging to Messrs Heins and Co, 'indefatigable caterers for the public in the matter of pianoforte and other instruments'. The Heins brothers, Nicholas and Ernest, organists at the churches of St Nicholas and All Saints, sold their wares from a showroom in Broad Street — two up from West Street — and from the aptly named Beethoven Hall in Berrington Street. Here, amid the celebrated Broadwoods, Bechsteins, Steinways and Bluthners, massed twelve rows deep, the partnership displayed their own 30 guinea pianoforte 'of great volume and tone, fitted with all the latest improvements' including brass candelabra. For greater cacophony 6 guineas would purchase their own parlour organ — 'certainly a little gem'. The 'long ecclesiastical looking hall admirably lighted with a number of Tudor windows', as the Berrington Street warehouse was described, was the defunct Countess of Huntingdon's chapel, erected in 1793 and abandoned in 1887 for a new church at the Crozens, Eign Road. In a way, the modulation of the Berrington Street building from chapel to 20th century bingo hall via a pianoforte warehouse admirably reflects social change during the last two centuries.

LEFT

George Heins, photographed in front of the Bishop's Palace, on his 80th birthday in March 1895. Mr Heins, who was born in Germany, founded Heins and Co in Broad Street after working 28 years for Broadwoods in London. In 1893 he would still 'tricycle' to the Heins shop in Brecon. He was highly regarded as an instrument restorer and in the same year re-built a spinet made in 1734.

RIGHT

A wonderful study of an Edwardian workman: a pipefitter with the Hereford Corporation Gas Works. W.H. Bustin, whose photographic studio was across the way in Palace Yard, obviously could not resist this stubbly artisan, especially when posed against the noble gatehouse usually reserved as the background for his photographs of the gentry and their equipages.

The Hereford Brewery of Messrs Watkins and Sons was founded in 1834 at the far end of Bewell Street, on a site 'favoured in possessing an excellent supply of the purest water from the famous Bewell spring'. In 1892 the company possessed 200 outlets, including 70 tied houses, principally in Birmingham and Hereford. Its leading products included Old Hereford Ale, National Household Ale, Watkins Cream Stout, Porter and, most famous of all — Golden Sunlight Ale which, according to an advertisement, had received the 'encomiums of many of the highest medical authorities' including Sir C. Cameron, MD, who said 'Golden Sunlight Ale resembles in appearance fine sherry'. It tasted rather like a lager. Beyond the proud rusticated gatepiers, where three vehicles are waiting to be loaded, two lines of granite steps for iron bound wheels lead through the brewery, past the bottle store on the right into the coopers' yard adjoining Wall Street.

CENTRE

The local delivery cart of Messrs Watkins Imperial Brewery sets out from the Monarch Works in Bewell Street c1890. The portly drayman, fattened by treats from grateful landlords, braces himself bashfully while the master's son, Alfred Watkins, takes a photograph. The battered bowler, knotted kerchief and leather apron are worn as symbols of his trade.

BELOW

The Golden Sunlight girl — the Ophelia of pale ale — shades her eyes from the incandescent glare of Messrs Watkins and Sons' award winning beverage.

LEFT

The other part of the Watkins empire, the Imperial Flour Mills in Friar Street from the sidings. The children have popped through the fence from Foundry Row, a group of cottages built by Capt Radford for his workers c1830. The great chimney also belonged to the Foundry, and in its day was regarded as one of the engineering wonders of Hereford. It was designed by James Prout, a shipwright and assistant to Radford, who later helped Stephen Ballard in the construction of the Hereford and Gloucester canal.

GOLDEN SUNLIGHT

Keep the
Golden
Sunlight
in your house
it is a light
pale Golden
Ale of pleasant
flavour & wonder-
-ful value. it is good,
it is light it is pure you will

like it better
than the
stronger
Burton Ale
and it will
not disagree
with you
Charles Watkins & Son
The Hereford Brewery
(Established 1834)

PALE ALE

COMPARE IT WITH OTHER BEERS.
"—MATCHED WITH MINE
ARE AS MOONLIGHT UNTO SUNLIGHT,
AND AS WATER UNTO WINE" Tennyson.

A view of the flour mill, photographed in 1903. Originally the two storey building on the left 'designed with simple taste and dignity which has not been equalled since in the Herefordshire manufacturing premises' (*Hereford Journal* 24 July 1915) housed the Hereford Foundry, established by Captain Radford in 1827. The superb ornamental balcony in front of the Old Mitre Hotel in Broad Street was cast here in 1836. C1850 the premises were bought by Charles Watkins of Wilcroft, Lugwardine, who added a malt house and a flour mill to supply the raw material for the Hereford Brewery in Bewell Street. When the Hereford and Shrewsbury railway was opened in December 1853, 500 navvies were entertained in the old foundry on 'tables groaning with huge joints and quarts of beer'.

A fine study of the great steam engine at the Imperial Mills; one of the innovations introduced by Alfred Watkins when he took over the mills was a dynamo, which produced the first electric light in Hereford in 1876.

Another innovation — a steam waggon being loaded at the Mills in 1905. The Imperial Mills produced a famous brown loaf called 'Vagos' which had the roughage excluded from the flour but still contained the wheat germ. The loaf was exhibited in London and sold widely in the West Midlands. Alfred Watkins debated the qualities of the loaf in a national health magazine at the beginning of the century. It disappeared after the Great War.

Like so many of Alfred Watkins' compositions, the 'dressing of the millstone' has a lyrical quality, which sets it apart from other photographs. The imagery has a Pre-Raphaelite clarity. Presumably Watkins, on one of his photographic sorties around the Friar Street mills which belonged to his family, came across this millwright quietly chasing new stones in an annexe to the works. Bright daylight from the open door illuminates his studied craftsmanship and the camera captures forever a world of meaningful labour.

The Herefordshire Beekeepers' Association was founded in 1882 at the height of the agricultural depression. One of its objectives was to popularise the culture of bees among the rural poor, as a means of augmenting their income and providing a free source of much-needed nourishment. Instruction classes were organised in the winter, and a horse-drawn Bee Van, fitted out for lantern slide shows, toured the countryside in the summer. Here a mainly juvenile audience watch a demonstration outside the Kite's Nest Inn at Stretton Sugwas. The Association was eager to promote the framed hive rather than the traditional plaited straw skep — both are shown here.

RIGHT

A certain amount of quality control was exercised by the Beekeepers' Association, who organised a weekly stall for honey and wax in the Hereford Butter Market. The stall, enhanced with parlour palm and posies was an object of pride for the neat girls in the photograph. In the background a basket maker displays his craft, and the broadsheets on the wall urge passers-by to read the sporting pages of the *Hereford Times* — the scene has changed little to-day.

BELOW

In 1906 Charles Hatton — on the far right of the photograph — sold the Barton Tannery and thus brought to a close an important chapter in the commercial history of Hereford. Fifty years earlier his family also worked the tanyards on the Tan Brook in Widemarsh Street Without but, as with so many other provincial industries, the railways encouraged centralisation and, in the absence of a thriving glove- or shoe-making trade to receive the products of the tanyards as, for instance, at Worcester, the industry was doomed to decay. Mr Hatton's workers stand amid the concrete tanpits or 'handlers', and hold various types of equipment for 'throwing up' the hides, which spent 12-18 months in and out of the bark liquor. On the left is the drying shed with movable shutters which, during warm weather, allowed for the circulation of ample air. In the winter the shed was warmed by hot water pipes.

Down Gwynne Street the brave English workman is leaning nonchalantly against his cart. The trench is clearly out of bounds for one so skilled. The foreman, top-hatted and every inch a gentleman, has his hands in his pockets for the duration of the exposure. In 1894 the Corporation improved their gas works at Holmer by introducing 'the regenerator system of heating the retorts' which, together with the adoption of the penny-in-the-slot system, resulted in a considerable increase in consumers. In Gwynne Street the assembled children are already dreaming of the hot dinners which the new fuel would provide. In the foreground, a boy falls to his knees to observe more closely the source of the flickering blue god. The sheds just visible at the top of the street indicate that the photograph was taken during the reconstruction of the west end of the Cathedral between 1902-8.

Aladdin's cave: the interior of Mr W. Margrett's shop, practical watchmaker and silversmith, in Broad Street where 'the display is so striking, the arrangements so elaborate and the glittering stock so suggestive of opulence and well-filled purses'. Margrett's class 'A' demi-hunter watches were guaranteed not to vary more than one second a week, while the modest silver 'Geneva' was recommended for schoolboys. As one of the leading horologists in Herefordshire, Mr Margrett specialised in making and erecting turret and church clocks, several of which could be seen in the county c1900. He was also the special optician to the recently established Herefordshire Eye Institution.

The foundation date of 1866 was proclaimed with pride upon the elaborate bill-heads of Augustus C. Edwards, draper, milliner, costumier and latterly, complete funeral furnishers and coffin makers. Alban House, which still graces High Town, with its swish Neo-classical facade, was probably designed for Mr Edwards by William Startin, the architect of the Green Dragon. In style it casts an eye towards the Paris of the Second Empire; the source, according to the proprietor, of the *modes* and fashions which excited his aristocratic *clientele*. As a 'county emporium of superior class' the shop provided 'fashionable novelties', generally regarded as the 'peculiar privilege of the residents of the metropolis'. We are told in 1892 that the 'handsome frontage of the shop with its six spacious plate glass windows was the most notable feature of the city's leading thoroughfare'. French and British dress fabrics; Spitalfields and oriental silks; seal, beaver, bear, squirrel, kangaroo, opossum, otter, musquash — virtually the complete fauna of the colonies — were available within the establishment which, naturally, 'paid most careful regard to sanitation'.

Mr T.A. King, monumental sculptor, was 'one of the celebrities of the ancient city'. Between 1877-92 he executed commissions in 130 churches in Herefordshire and his monuments can be found as far afield as Devon, Lancashire and Oxford. Perhaps his most familiar work is the Triumphal Arch which forms the Venn memorial in Commercial Road, erected in 1891. There are also a number of elaborate canopies and figured tombs at Belmont and the Cemetery. His monumental works in Eign Street — on the site of the Victoria Street subway — was suitably 'adorned with appropriate carvings giving a foretaste of what may be seen within'. Mr King also carried out estimates for architects, was an expert photographer and a modeller in clay. 'A bust of a Pompeian lady in his studio is a masterpiece of modelling . . . suggestive of the work of an eminent sculptor' — so a correspondent claimed in 1892.

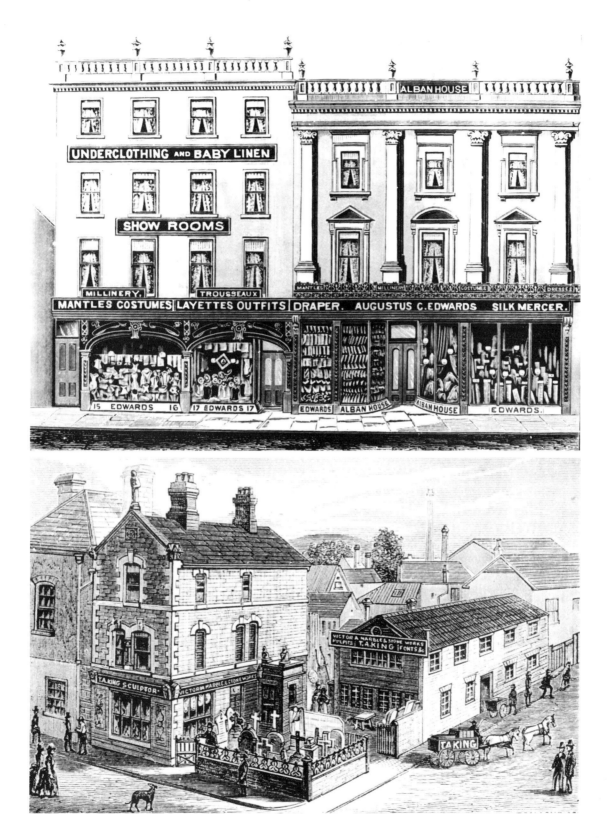

A gloomy winter's day at the Cattle Market, where a special sale seems to be in progress; not animals, but perhaps Christmas fare. The site is now occupied by the retail market. The corrugated iron sale ring is a familiar landmark, but not here. It must have been moved to the site it occupied until 1979. In the background the bare elms of Richmond Place stand in a quiet suburb, unscarred c1920 by modern traffic.

This market scene at the beginning of the century is still familiar, but the setting has changed considerably. The last of the great cast iron stanchions, very much in evidence here, disappeared from the old pens beneath the horse chestnuts in 1978. In the background there are two of the original market buildings erected in 1856 — the weigh-house and the fruit market. Houses still cluster thickly in New Market Street.

It is c1900 and possibly Sunday. All Hereford's citizens are at home, Little Church Street is deserted, but Mr Adams poses for W.H. Bustin before the family business in High Town. To relieve the gloom of a damp day, the incandescent gas lamps are burning, throwing a cheerful light upon the assorted wares on display. Printing seems to be a minor part of the firm's activities, for the windows are full of 'English and foreign toys', picture frames and ornaments. Above, two panels of Glacier stained glass — a nice Victorian touch — are attached to the first floor windows. Boots, with an eye to the rural world beyond High Town are selling 'Sheep Dip Powder' — for cash, of course.

Edward George arrived in Hereford with the canal in 1845. He already had a timber yard at Withington — for a few years in the 1840s the terminus of the Hereford and Gloucester Canal — and another at Etnam Street, Leominster. The alliance with Mr Tudor came in the 1870s but, as this photograph taken at an agricultural show c1890 indicates, the old name was retained for some time afterwards. Then the company was the 'principal emporium' for building materials of all sorts with stocks of 'roofing slates from Port Madoc and Penrhyn quarries, Broseley and Bridgwater roofing tiles, blue Staffordshire goods, garden tiles, facing and paving bricks &c' all of which contributed to the wonderful diversity of Hereford's buildings.

Monkmoor Mills in Commercial Road, now a furniture warehouse, belonged in the Middle Ages to the monastery of St Guthlac, across the road on the site of the County Hospital. The corn mill was driven by a head of water drawn from the Smalpors or Tan Brook, which was culverted from the Eign Brook in the Merton Medows. In the late 19th century, the mill belonged to Messrs Herron and Son, a London firm of woolmerchants, who abandoned it for 'a powerful engine with four large boilers'. A new workshop, illustrated in the photograph, was erected on a site facing the street, part of which had been occupied 1825-1880 by the Hereford Gas Works. For a short time Monkmoor became the centre of an international enterprise served, of course, by the railway just around the corner. Raw sheep skins were brought from Australia and, after being scoured, cleansed, combed, dried and pulled from the hides, the pure wool was sent to the company's warehouse near London Bridge, where it was supplied to 'manufacturers in all the great centres of the woollen industry'. The skins were steeped in limepits, drenched and transformed into leather, the best of which was sent to the glovers of Yeovil and Worcester while 'a number of inferior skins were prepared for the American market'. The millpool behind the factory, although no longer used for power, provided copious water for many of the processes and survived until the early 20th century.

It could well be Oxford Street, but it is Hereford — an unidentified shop window, possibly Augustus C. Edwards and Sons Ltd, High Town. With a magnifying glass the date 1920 can be read on the advertisements. Gone is the austerity of the War years, the 'gay' '20s have arrived and Hereford's women are treated to an extravagant display of exotic dresses. Flared skirts, which gave fashion-conscious working women mobility during the War, are ousted by the tubular 'barrel line' — flat busts, boyish cocquetry and ostrich plumes are the order of the day.

It could be Broadway in 1922 but it is Broad Street, Hereford. The prominent sign above the porch indicates that the Green Dragon Hotel had adapted to the motor car age, but the pigeons on the road suggest that the traffic was far from continuous.

But for the plate glass windows, this is one of the finest Late Georgian houses in Hereford. To-day Clyde House School faces the A49 traffic island in Edgar Street, but in 1900 it was surrounded by gardens, gated and enclosed in the manner of London squares, a suitable environment for a boarding and day school 'old established, well reputed, accessible to day boys with home comforts for boarders' where 'sound commercial education, shorthand and book-keeping, music and fine arts, cricket and football' formed the basis of the curriculum. Mr J. Lingham-Lees, BA, Lond was the headmaster, assisted by 'competent resident and visiting masters'. The lace curtains and trimmed blinds are a special period feature, as is the great wisteria which has been replaced to-day by an equally impressive Virginia creeper.

RIGHT

Not the Petrograd Soviet waiting for news of the storming of the Tsar's palace but the editorial staff of the *Hereford Times* posing in difficult circumstances for W.H. Bustin c1900. The braced positions of the figures suggest a long exposure was necessary. The room was probably above the presses in Maylord Street, where the paper was printed by 'electric power'. This novelty — indicated by the pear-shaped light bulbs — was introduced in 1899. The telephone, obviously the real subject of this photograph, arrived the year before, when the National Telephone Company erected an exchange in East Street. When the Post Office took the system over in 1906 there were 110 telephones in Hereford. The editor is poised with his hand on the appliance.

BELOW

Frank Richardson, Chief Constable of the Hereford City Police, poses like some Arthurian knight on his white stallion before the craggy facade of the Police Station in Gaol Street.

The new automatic telephone system installed on the first floor of the Post Office in Broad Street increased the capacity of the Hereford exchange to 500 subscribers. To bring in these lines great posts were erected close to the exchange. One of these is going up behind Gwynne Street in 1913. The Post Office engineers, encouraged perhaps by the admiring glances of the young women on the tin roof, regarded this feat as an occasion for display and arranged themselves in hazardous positions for W.H. Bustin, who had carried his camera up into Rogers and Co's grain store behind Bridge Street. The attractive pantiled buildings, clustering behind Palace Yard — one of them partly timber-framed — belonged to the Spread Eagle in King Street. Just visible, under the corrugated iron roof, was Bustin's studio.

In 1849 the tragic death of a servant girl in Widemarsh Street convinced the City Council that Hereford needed a fire brigade. Twelve part-time men 'with a knowledge of buildings' were recruited and placed under the control of the superintendent of police. The local insurance companies contributed to the cost of the brigade and periodically checked its effectiveness. In 1910 it was regarded as one of the most efficient in the West Midlands. Initially the engine and ladders were kept under the Old Town Hall in High Town but, in 1875, a 'shed' was reconditioned as a fire station in Gaol Street. Five years later a steam pump was purchased from Sandringham — Queen Victoria's country house in Norfolk — for £574 16s. Re-named the *Nell Gwynne* it is seen here together with a manual pump in Cantilupe Street. This street was created in 1883 and the pegs in the foreground presumably mark the plots of the new houses. Behind, Miss Musgrave's greenhouse looks over the ivy-covered wall of Castle Pool House, across a piece of delightfully untamed waste ground.

The staff of the General Hospital photographed just before the First World War. The dog perched upon the head of the Chairman of the Board of Management seems to be an alien ingredient in the antiseptic environment of a hospital — even then. The white bows of the nurses, part of their qualifying insignia, clearly indicate a certain amount of self-expression. The nurse in the centre-right of the photograph, who is apparently supported by the doctor behind, has one, with some especially fine trimmings.

PLAYTIME

ABOVE

The Half Moon Inn in Broad Street: said to be 1856 but surely a little later. One imagines the photographer was one of those ardent young disciples of Ruskin, scouring the borderland for the timbers of old England, but such was the novelty of his equipment — or perhaps his intentions — Mr Bannister's taproom emptied onto the pavement. The result: one of the most atmospheric photographs of Hereford — the past is given warmth, crumpled trousers, stained waistcoats and all. Above the figures the decrepit building, daub crumbling and bressummer sinking, is about to be squeezed out of existence by its swish Neo-classical neighbours. Yet, by some remarkable chance it survived: a complete 16th century structure with mediaeval cellars and an enriched early Stuart ceiling hidden today beneath a plaster veneer. Thus, one can only regret the loss of the hand-painted inn sign — and, of course, the pub and its jolly patrons.

LEFT

At atmospheric view of the best room in the Bunch of Grapes, East Street. Every city has a pub in which there is a brown, smoke-stained room where townsmen have met for centuries — a room like this, lined with refined but sticky deal panelling, heavily moulded where it meets the ochre coloured ceiling. Around the walls are firmly fixed seats with turned legs, the varnish on the arms scuffed away by Georgian and Victorian cuffs, their backs canvas-lined and hair-stuffed. Two multi-light windows with recessed shutter boxes provide a dim light from the narrow street outside. A mirror, a ticking clock, a few ashtrays — on the floor, of course — a polished table or two and a cavernous fireplace provide the sparse setting for conversation anointed with liquor from the bar next door — a well adjusted man's world. The room is still there but the men are younger, their elders having retreated to the sub-urban pubs. There are women here too.

RIGHT

In 1901 the Hereford Bowling Club won all its home matches and was looking forward to a visit by a New Zealand team in the following year. These photographs, with the Union flags flying from the billiard room windows, were probably taken during the tour.

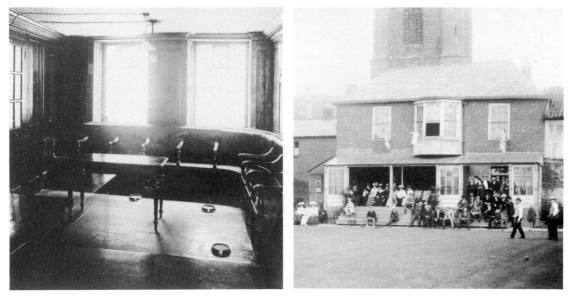

It is reassuring to know that the Hereford Bowling Club house, built in the mid-18th century, remains exactly like this to-day. Only the parlour palms, the lime tree and the houses in Bewell Street are absent. According to tradition, the club should hold its quincentenary celebrations in 1984 on what is, perhaps, the oldest green in England — a living monument.

Without these enthusiasts a book like this would be impossible. The Herefordshire Photographic Society posed with their cumbersome equipment on the terrace steps at Goodrich Court. To the fore, Harold Moffatt Esq, their host, and the president of the Society, J. Blake Esq. Unlike the Woolhope Club then, the photographers seem to have welcomed women on their outings. Like 'cycling, the new art of photography was enthusiastically embraced by women to support their claims of intrinsic equality. Alfred Watkins, bearded and bowler-hatted, stands holding his camera in the middle of the group.

This interesting photograph of High Town, taken in the 1920s, shows that it was still possible for the town to act as host to the countryside. The Mid-Herefordshire Hunt could meet in the centre of Hereford without too much inconvenience to traffic and, no doubt, still expect to raise a fox in the fields above Barrs Court or in the countryside beyond the Bishop's Meadows. That such a large crowd gathered in the rain implies an infrequent event or perhaps the town was full of Saturday morning shoppers. Clearly, the most sensible place to be was in Pritchard's parlour or Messrs Kings' first floor fitting room.

BELOW

In the first week of September 1904, Hereford experienced an 'invasion of horseless carriages' to which, in the stylish journalese of the local paper, the citizens only 'offered passive resistance'. The Automobile Club of Great Britain and Ireland used Hereford as a base for their sixth annual road trials, for cars with a purchase price of less than £200. The City Council was initially hesitant, but the prospect of numerous well-off visitors and the knowledge that 'at present Ross was almost a centre for motor cars, while Hereford was left out in the cold' tipped the balance. As a gesture of goodwill it offered the 60-70 competitors a dinner but, being practical men, the trial organisers asked for the loan of the Drill Hall to accommodate their pampered vehicles overnight, and facilities in the Cattle Market for car washing. The event passed without mishap, although Dinmore Hill apparently claimed a number of blown engines and, on Wednesday, as cattle converged upon Hereford market, the old world met the new, causing a certain amount of conflict on the narrow county lanes. The climax arrived on Saturday with a grand parade through the City led by Miss Levill in her De Dion. She had captured the hearts of competitors and spectators alike and received a daring tribute at the Town Hall of red roses from the bashful Mayor, Alderman Charles Witts.

Members of the Herefordshire Automobile Club proudly displayed their new toys in the Palace Yard. The president, Mr J.T. Hereford of Sufton was responsible for bringing the trials to Hereford in 1904. The masons' lodge in front of the new west end of the Cathedral suggests a date of 1902-3.

RIGHT

In contrast to the coarse and heavyweight build of the early automobiles, in style closely related to the broad-wheeled farm cart, this flyweight vehicle, with its economy of materials, refined lines and sinuous curves, represents the zenith of the carriage builder's art.

CENTRE LEFT

'Are we on the right road for Hereford?' Two young men, fully dressed for the coarse sport of long distance motor 'cycling, pose on their Coventry-made machines in the outdoor extension to Bustin's studio in Palace Yard. The heavy bag and Union pennant on CB-632 suggest that this photograph was taken on the eve of an expedition abroad — perhaps to Wales?

BELOW

February 1917 — throughout England the major rivers froze, including rapid streams such as the Wye. According to the *Hereford Journal* the river 'was thronged with hundreds of persons' attracted by 'a splendid piece of ice from the boathouse up'. It provided the war-weary citizens with 'several hours of relaxation'. In this photograph the throng seems to have dispersed. At Huntington Pool, however, the scene was more joyous. The Edwardian era saw the climax of the skating craze — even Hereford had a rink in Eign Street; thus most people could put their hands upon some skates. There had been little snow in Hereford but heavy falls had been reported 13-14 miles away.

LEFT

The Hereford Rowing Club Regatta was held on the third Saturday in July with the Shrewsbury, Tewkesbury, Worcester and Bath clubs competing for the West of England challenge vase. The parasols suggest that this was indeed one of those halcyon days before the First World War. How much less canal-like the river Wye appears. Its banks, gently crumbling towards the river, provided a gradation of viewpoints for the spectators and many convenient anchorages for boats. As with other views of the river during this period, the number of rowing boats calls for comment. Where did they all go? Today there is hardly a clinker-built boat to be seen in the vicinity of Hereford.

RIGHT AND CENTRE

Under the wall of the General Hospital, sprouting drain pipes like some Crimean redoubt, two well-dressed women and their children, also in Sunday best, pause to look at some natural wonder in the shingle beside the Wye. How they would have loved to have been able to cross the river at this point on the Victoria Bridge which was to be erected in 1897. Behind, near the solitary man, is a rough wall which originally formed the dam for the pool of the castle mill. The second photograph, taken slightly earlier, shows the yawning holes of the Mill Street culverts. At anchor is the *Princess Mary* ferry boat and its proprietress. How full of trees Hereford was in the late 19th century. A bunch of great elms dominated Castle Cliffe.

BELOW

The Castle Cliffe looking decidedly bosky and untamed in this photograph, taken before the building of the Victoria Bridge (1897). The dignified Doric portico erected by the Society of Tempers in 1778 and its adjoining coffee house/bath suite produce a composition close to the aesthetic aspirations of a generation who admired the paintings of Poussin, Claude and Salvator Rosa. The utilitarian additions to the Old Coffee House and the recent engineering work upon the Cliff have considerably reduced the 'picturesque' qualities of this outstanding piece of urban landscape.

91

The May Fair attracted almost as many early photographers as the Cathedral. These photographs, presumably taken from a first-floor window on the north side of High Town, perfectly capture the enchantment of the occasion. Unlike its shadow today, the fair in 1890 was essentially an adult entertainment, bringing twopenny pleasures to the hard-working and under-stimulated population of Hereford. From these pictures it seems it was also a daylight affair, and the atmosphere of these views — especially the fine array of straw hats — suggests a Saturday afternoon. There is nothing twilit about this crowd. The hard core of Hereford's citizens are present. There is also a strong feeling of theatre, not far removed from similar occasions in the Middle Ages, with barkers and dancing girls cajoling and enticing the curious to part with their money, and to taste the magic arts of the gilded paradise within.

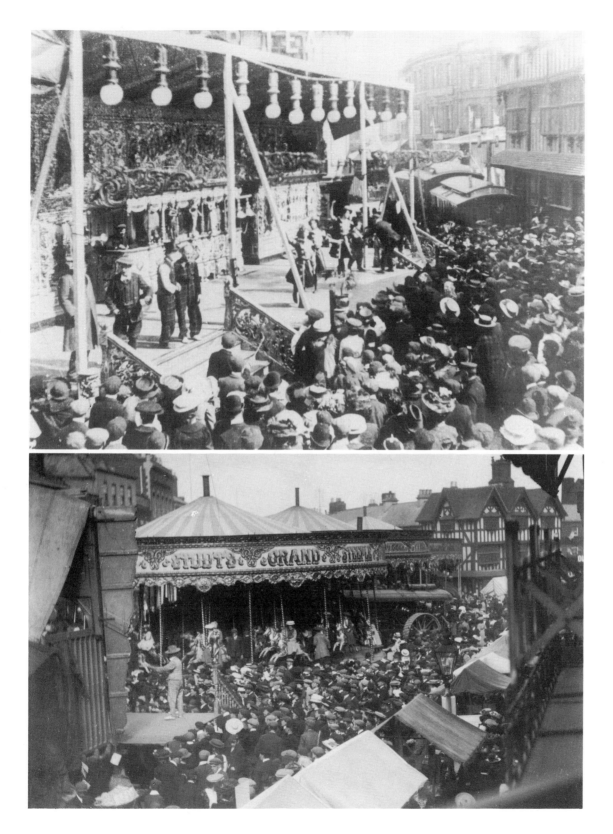

The May Fair in 1912 which, according to the *Hereford Journal* demonstrated that 'the good old days are still with us in spirit, if not in exact semblance'. Like Tennyson's brook 'it keeps on running and there are appears no sign yet of its passing away from the disease known as old age'.

It was rather quiet at 5.00 pm when the first photograph was taken but the *Journal* reporter anticipated that the electric lights and 'town element' would soon waken things up a bit. By 8.00 pm 'the evening air was rent with laughter and shouting which could be heard in spite of the combined forces of blazing trumpets, the clamour of bells, the raucous cries of the showmen and above all the strident tones of organs in keen and never ceasing competition'. Notwithstanding the declamations of the 'superior ones' the *Journal* felt 'the neat and natty atire' of the dancers was an advance on previous years. However, the simulation of the last hours of the *Titanic* was disappointing, while the man eating shark was 'as old as the ark' and Lady Dot 'a lady of uncertain age but certainly small'. Also, more sensational than pleasing was the Englishman dressed as an Indian, who placed a handful of snakes in his mouth.

Apparently, 'switches and squirts' had been banned by the Council but bags of confetti used as missiles, especially when replenished from the gutter, were also 'beyond a joke' if you were a recipient. Meanwhile, in the Temperance tent the Dean delivered a thoughtful address comparing the 1600 lives lost on the *Titanic* with the 100,000 lost each year through drink. On the following morning the justices were busy prosecuting pick-pockets from West Bromwich and the proprietor of a coconut shy, who defeated his patrons by filling his nuts with lead. He was fined £5.

RIGHT

Broad Street emerges once again as another May Fair is hauled away in a great broad wheeled farm-cart. A rather bent citizen surveys the debris, and one of the revellers seems to be trussed up in the foreground — or is it just a tent bag?

BELOW

A mystery photograph. From its placing in the Bustin Collection this is the May Fair camped outside Hereford c1910, waiting for permission to enter the City. The bosky setting seems familiar but it is difficult to place it. The Georgian house in the background should provide a useful clue. Is it below the Tupsley ridge adjoining the Lugg Meadows or, perhaps, beside the Wye at Broomy Hill? It is certainly a photograph with a great deal of atmosphere.

ABOVE AND CENTRE
A sure sign that the circus was in town was the regular afternoon dip below Castle Cliffe of performing horses and occasionally more exotic beasts, such as elephants or zebras. The headlong drive through the city from Widemarsh Common was bound to create a festive atmosphere, and attract a large crowd of would-be circus goers. Happily, the setting has hardly changed — Castle Cliffe, is perhaps less 'gothick' without its creeper and the public slip is not so accessible, but Hereford's great quay wall below Vaga House is still intact. One might also regret the loss of the intimate landscape of trimmed hedges which surrounded the nursery on the site of the Redcliffe gardens.

BELOW
Hereford celebrated Queen Victoria's Diamond Jubilee with great enthusiasm on Tuesday, 22 June 1897. 'The pageant', claimed the *Hereford Journal,* 'will, if the weather is auspicious, be one that will entirely dwarf all other past local displays'. Fortunately, 'Queen's weather' prevailed throughout the celebrations and umbrellas, brought in anticipation of rain, were used as parasols. It was so hot, the chairman of the organising committee, Mr Phillips, 'was siezed of an attack of sun-stroke whilst parading' and thus missed the Grand Procession which he had rehearsed so carefully. The day began with the hoisting of a massive Union Jack, nearly 30ft long, on a 54ft staff attached to the Cathedral tower, and ended with bonfires and fireworks on Castle Green, where an illuminated portrait of the Queen formed a fitting *finalé*. From Aylestone Hill it was possible to see 38 bonfires on distant high-points, including the greatest of all erected by John Hungerford Arkwright on Henhouse Bank above Hampton Court.

LEFT

On 13 May 1902, Princess Henry of Battenberg — Princess Beatrice, Victoria's youngest daughter and life-long companion — visited Hereford to unveil the Women's Memorial Window in the Cathedral to her august mother, and also to lay the foundation stone of the new Town Hall. The Princess was guest of the Earl and Countess of Chesterfield and so approached the City from Holme Lacy. Hereford, apparently, had an 'unwontedly gay appearance', not least because of the several arches erected over the Princess's route. This one in St Martin's — 'a structure of grand proportions and quite in keeping with the architecture of the ancient Wye Bridge' — was inscribed 'Welcome to our City'. Along with a further 'corinthian structure' in St Peter's Street, it was paid for by Messrs Greenlands Ltd. The flock of sheep approaching the arch out of the mist was presumably not part of the procession.

RIGHT

Princess Beatrice, escorted by the Herefordshire troop of the Shropshire Imperial Yeomanry, is greeted by a huge crowd in King Street. 'Many ominous clouds threatened to discharge their burden' but fortunately, the day turned out to be dry but cold. The County Volunteers 'lent the necessary touch of colour to the scene' for 'not within recent years, if at all, have the streets of the city been lined with the military'. The arrival of the Princess was heralded by a party of military 'cyclists — England's secret weapon against the Boers. Quite a lot has changed on the north side of King Street, where not a shop front is visible. Then it was one of Hereford's principal residential streets.

BELOW

The boys of the Cathedral School decorated the west gates of the Close with evergreens, to produce a further 'ocular expression' of loyalty to the Princess. The Castle Street gates received similar treatment, but crossed oars replaced the reverent inscription cast in bold red letters. Above the houses flags droop from the scaffolding erected before the Memorial Window. The state of the street suggests that the photograph was taken early in the morning, before the City scavengers had set to work. W.H. Bustin had been invited to Holme Lacy the evening before, where he had 'secured a truly magnificent group'. A proof presented to the Princess during lunch at the Bishop's Palace was 'greatly admired'.

A great crowd throngs the grandstand at the racecourse to greet the French air ace M Salmet on Saturday, 20 July 1912. Sponsored by the *Daily Mail,* M Salmet had spent the summer hopping across southern England, demonstrating the amazing qualities of his Bleriot monoplane. At Hereford, the French-built machine, with its 50 hp Gnome engine, flew so low over the spectators it made them duck. On landing, the crowd surged forward to write their signatures on the plane's canvas frame, while the pilot was carried off to tea with Sir Archer Croft and Sir Geoffrey Cornewall. The night was spent at The Firs, Hampton Park, the house of the Mayor, Alderman Wallis, and early the next morning, after complimenting Hereford on being a clean and beautiful City, M. Salmet flew on to Worcester. *En route* a storm brought him down in a field near Broadheath, thus disappointing the large crowd gathered on the Malverns. Such was the atmosphere of those innocent days of early technology — perhaps not so innocent since M Salmet's plane, we are told, was built for military service.

The unveiling of the statue of Sir George Cornewall Lewis by the Prime Minister, Lord Palmerston outside the Shirehall in 1863. Few people realise to-day that, but for his premature death at the age of 56, Sir George would probably have succeeded Palmerston as leader of the Liberal Party.

On a cold January afternoon in 1906, the prospective Conservative parliamentary candidate for Hereford, 'the young and popular squire of Hampton Court', John S. Arkwright addresses the electorate from the balcony of the Mitre Hotel in Broad Street. A few days later the Liberals won a sweeping victory throughout the country, bringing to an end twenty years of Conservative government. In Hereford, however, a deferential vote, aided, according to the Liberals by 'treating and bribery', denied victory to their candidate, Col Lucas Scudamore. William Collins, the leading propagandist of the defeated party, reflected bitterly that 'The city of Hereford has failed in its parliamentary duty . . . the lying spirit of a general election spreads its wings over the nation and permeates all classes and conditions alike'. Referring to Arkwright he admitted 'The man is right enough, it is his political opinions which are wrong'.

A remarkably fine array of mutton-chops and stove-pipes from the members of the Herefordshire Agricultural Society (est 1789), as they pose on the balcony of the Grandstand at the racecourse. The building itself had obviously seen better days. Occasionally, less sedate events took place in the Assembly Room, which resulted in broken windows.

LEFT

A 'grand masonic function' took place in Hereford on Tuesday, 14 May 1907 when the Right Honourable and Right Worshipful Earl of Warwick, past deputy Grand Master of England, laid the foundation stone for one of the turrets at the West End of the Cathedral. Here the Hereford Palladian Lodge of Ancient Free and Accepted Masons (f 1762) marched with aprons, sashes and other accoutrements through High Town. Remarkably most of the buildings — at least above the ground floor — can be recognised to-day. Wakefield Knight surely deserve a prize for remaining steadfast throughout the greater part of the 20th century. Looming over the scene like some great totem is the telegraph pole which marked the site of the first telephone exchange in East Street.

RIGHT

A rather small crowd in St Peter's Square watch a contingent of the Welsh Border Brigade and the civic party as they pass the scaffolding surrounding the site of St Peter's Church House, the foundation stone for which had been laid the previous week. According to the *Journal* reporter 'a profusion of flags and buntings met the eye in each direction'. The Queen, however, may not have been amused by the banner on the Commercial Inn (now the Halfcrown) in Commercial Road which read 'Well played 60 and not out' and invited passers by to 'Honour the Queen and step in and drink her health'.

BELOW

According to the legend on this negative, this is the garden of 31 Castle Street, showing the Dean of Hereford and his family. In fact it is 2 Castle Street, which was occupied c1900 by Miss Mary Carless, while the Dean was the Very Rev the Hon James Wentworth Leigh, DD. Regardless of personalities, the photograph is full of significant period detail. Notice especially the elaborate oil burner keeping the kettle warm — not recommended for windy days on the Malverns — and the multi-position cake stand, supporting the definitive Edwardian fruit cake. The bashful young man seems to have outgrown his chair but presumably he is still a child in the eyes of his mother. The dog, like all dogs in all ages, is treating the occasion with characteristic disdain.

A fine array of hats, caps, bowlers and boaters in the Castle Green c1900. Some of the adults find the photographer far more interesting than the Punch and Judy show.

Hereford's secret weapon: the women's section of the Herefordshire Bow Meeting going through their paces at the Militia Barracks in Harold Street, on the eve of the First World War. The elaborate belt fitting, clasping the wasp-like waist of the participant in the foreground, suggests there were champions here. In the centre one of the competitors whirls with Dervish-like euphoria as she recoils from releasing her arrow, too fast for the camera's primitive shutter. Rather suitably, in the presence of such magnificence, the men in attendance are engaged in menial tasks, like keeping score, holding equipment etc. In the background two boys lie low on the wall, stunned by this Atlantaean display of the martial arts.

'H.M.S. Jubilee' the leading float in the Police and City Council section of the Grand Procession ready to move off from Victoria Street. This street has changed dramatically since 1968, but the cottages on the left confirm the identification. Other themes included in the procession were: 'Defence of the Colours'; 'The Progress of Agriculture'; 'The Progress of Road Locomotion' led by a motor car lent by Messrs Lever Brothers of Port Sunlight and 'Electricity' — a joint tableau presented by the Fire Brigade and the Hereford Working Boys.

The scene on Castle Green at 3.30 pm, with the massed choirs of the city schools singing patriotic songs, conducted by Dr George Robinson Sinclair, the Cathedral organist. 'Quite enchanting' was the verdict of the *Hereford Journal.* The occasion reached a climax when, at a signal from the conductor, the children produced flags to a 'good many hearty cheers'. Dr Sinclair went on to conduct an evening concert attended by 8-900 people. For those who had had enough of *Rule Britannia* and *Victoria Our Queen*, there was an Olde Englyshe Sports at Edgar Street promoted by the Football Club to clear its debts — a familiar problem.

Mrs Roland Bent, beneath the austere portico of Athelstan Hall, Aylestone Hill c1900. The house was built in the late 1880s, probably for the widowed Mrs Bent, who is the first occupant mentioned in directories. Miss Emily Bent, presumably one of the girls in the photograph, lived here in 1912, but in 1913 the house was empty, and soon after the War it was occupied by Thomas Leonard Lane, turf accountant. Everyone on this photograph is carefully posed in a hierarchical position. Primogeniture insists that the son should stand at the apex of the group, his hands placed awkwardly in his pockets in the manner of a gentleman. The eldest daughter sits in filial proximity to Mrs Bent, yet displays fashionable qualities which suggest she is of a marriageable disposition. The two youngest daughters occupy a peripheral position, which suitably reflects their status in the laws governing inheritance. It is just possible that one of them may still be alive to-day.

BY GRAND DESIGN

ABOVE

This illustration from John Clayton's *A Collection of Ancient Timber Framed Edifices of England* (1846) shows the Aubrey Almshouses in Berrington Street. They were built c1636, according to the will of Mrs Mary Price, in the grounds of Wroughtall House which stood behind the Green Dragon in Wroughtall Lane. The hospital presumably took its present name when Wroughtall Lane became Aubrey Street c1855. The building has changed little since Clayton's day, although the setting has been replaced. Clayton was a native of Hereford and designed the Butter Market campanile in 1861. His book, which also contained an illustration of the Old Market Hall, did a great deal to stimulate a new interest in the vernacular architecture of England, providing a prelude to the Arts and Crafts movement of the late 19th century. Notwithstanding Clayton's campaign to prevent the demolition of the Old Market Hall — he provided several detailed reconstruction drawings for its refurbishment — 'the most fantastic black and white building in England' (Pevsner) came down in 1862.

CENTRE

John Nash's County Gaol in Commercial Street on the eve of its demolition in 1930. Following a serious outbreak of gaol fever in 1783 and prompted by the prison reformers, a number of counties on the Oxford circuit began to rebuild their prisons in the late 18th century. In 1795 Hereford was one of the first. As an architect the magistrates chose John Nash who, following his bankruptcy in 1783, fled to Wales and had recently completed gaols at Carmarthen and Cardigan. He was also engaged in remodelling Kentchurch Court for John Scudamore, MP for Hereford, and enhancing the new, picturesque landscape at Belmont with ornée cottages for John Mathews, the Mayor of the City. The design for Hereford Gaol was similar to Cardigan, but derived ultimately from Newgate, built by George Dance, in 1769. The deeply rusticated stonework and heavy grilled openings became clichés of prison architecture in the 19th century, but in 1795 they were still rather novel. Originally the entrance was divided by two Greek Doric columns, the first sign of an idiom to be developed fully at the Shirehall a decade later. To-day, only the governor's house remains as a booking office; its public lavatories must be the only ones in England designed by the Prince Regent's architect.

RIGHT AND BELOW

The original scheme for the Broad Street front of St Francis Xavier is not quite the building that appears there to-day. As Pevsner remarks, with its two giant Greek Doric columns it 'is bewildering, and would have driven Pugin frantic had he known it'. But from this drawing, the architect Charles Day obviously intended something more conventional — a diminutive version of the Shirehall crowned with a correct but rather ungainly bellcote, rather than a pediment. The Shirehall may easily have been in Day's mind, for at this time (1837-8) he was supervising the construction of the new Shirehall at Worcester, where he was County Surveyor. Greek was a natural choice of style for a catholic chapel at this early date in the 19th century, emphasising the Hellenistic, rather than the unpopular Roman origins of the faith. The interior is decidedly utilitarian and non-conformist.

The Gloucestershire Bank, erected on the corner of High Street/Broad Street c1860, in architectural terms was something quite new to Hereford. The architects were Messrs Medland and Maberly of Gloucester, whose *tour de force* in their own city is the Eastgate Street market entrance. The gorgeous enrichments on the Hereford building were carved by James Forsyth of Worcester, perhaps better known for his work in 'beautifying' the great hall at Eastnor Castle, and the magnificent Perseus fountain at Great Witley. Unfortunately, the ground floor windows, with their polychrome arches and the superb entrance containing the arms of Hereford and Gloucester surrounded by oak and ivy foliage, were destroyed in 1928.

RIGHT

If Frederick Kempson had had his way, Holy Trinity Church, Whitecross Road would have boasted the finest spire in Hereford. Kempson of Widemarsh Street, the most prolific architect of late Victorian Herefordshire, was a noted spire builder with Coddington (1863), Wolferlow (1863), Tupsley (1865) and Pipe and Lyde (1874) already to his credit when Holy Trinity was opened in 1883 with neither spire nor chancel. The latter was eventually built in 1906, but to the designs of Nicholson and Hartree — old competitors of Kempson — in a 'slightly later decorated period than the nave' which, as the illustration from *The Builder* shows, was decidedly Early English — 13th century rather than 14th century. The church was built of a mixture of Three Elms, Fayre Oaks and Withington stone with stone enrichments by T.A. King, woodwork by Frank Dredge and tiles provided by Messrs Godwin & Co of Lugwardine. Lacking both chancel and spire, the eminent Victorian architectural historian H.S. Goodhart-Rendel called it, rather unfairly, 'the dullest design I have ever seen — not worth describing'. Fortunately, Kempson left St Paul's (1865), the City Library, Broad Street (1873) and the County College (1881) as positive evidence of his skills.

BELOW

A perspective view of the new Benedictine monastery and cathedral of St Michael and All Angels at Belmont — the soaring expression by Pugin and Pugin of the pious dreams of Francis Wegg-Prosser and Thomas Brown, OSB, the first catholic bishop of Newport. It is not quite the building that stands here to-day. This was completed in 1858, while this view was commissioned in 1878, when a new central tower was proposed, together with a chantry chapel to hold the body of Bishop Brown. The extensive Elizabethan-gothic claustral range looks less impressive to-day, and was designed and completed by Edward Welby Pugin in 1858. Until 1920, Belmont was the only English catholic cathedral governed by a bishop and a chapter of monks — like Worcester and a number of other English cathedrals before the Reformation. The contractor for the original work was Arthur Maggs of Hereford, who, having failed to provide a damp course, saw most of his work pulled down before completion. The fine sandstone came from Spring Grove in Haywood Forest, the same quarry that provided stone for Wye Bridge. The total cost of the work in 1859 was £45,000, £30,000 of which was provided by Francis Wegg-Prosser.

The age of steam had arrived for Hereford. This famous print of the iron bridge over the Wye at Hunderton was produced to celebrate the opening of the Newport, Abergavenny and Hereford Railway on 6 December 1853 — prematurely, as it happened, for a slip in a cutting at Llanfiangel Crucorney delayed the actual opening until 2 January 1854. The first train crossed the bridge to the still incomplete Barton Station, but failed to make the anticipated connection with the Shrewsbury and Hereford line, because of a lack of signals at Barrs Court Junction. Beneath the bridge, another wonder of the age — a steam pleasure boat belonging to Francis Wegg-Prosser of Belmont, which arrived in July 1853 via the Hereford and Gloucester canal.

CENTRE

Burghill Hospital or, to give it its 19th century name, the Hereford County and City Lunatic Asylum, is perhaps the largest and least appreciated High Victorian building in Herefordshire. Here it is as its creator, Robert Griffiths of Stafford, saw it in 1872, from an engraving printed in *The Builder* to celebrate its opening. The concept, of course, is a country house, and even the 'airing courts', laid out in a geometric form to complement the Italianate architecture of the building, convey a sense of rural privacy. Like most Victorian utilities, the asylum was an object of considerable pride for the local inhabitants. *Jakeman and Carver* declared categorically that 'The county and city of Hereford are in possession of one of the best and most complete asylums in England'. It accommodated 300 female and 250 male patients — an interesting ratio — who occupied 11 wards with 'extensive and beautiful views of the surrounding country'. Each ward had two bathrooms. The twin campanile, flanking a first floor chapel and a hall for stage plays and dances, provided a focus for the building and gave it a distant skyline rather like Osborne House. Surrounding the asylum there was a 100 acre farm, the profit from which 'diminishes the cost per week of the patients more than perhaps any other asylum'. The death rate in 1902 was the lowest in England and in the first 30 years only one case of suicide had occurred.

ABOVE

Regarded as one of the 'leading schools' in the area, the Hereford County College on Aylestone Hill was erected at a cost of £17,000 in 1881. It was also known as the School of Science, Commerce and Agriculture, and thus appealed to the middle ranks of county society, who wanted an education for their children based upon 'modern principles'. This ideal was close to the heart of Sir James Rankin of Bryngwyn, a benefactor of the school and chairman of its governors until its demise, following the 1902 Education Act. The fees c1900 for day boys were £10 per annum, for boarders £40. The architect was F.R. Kempson of Hereford, a prolific church restorer and whose City Library in Broad Street was another product of Sir James Rankin's generosity. As befits a scholastic building it is soberly gothic, but the use of polychrome brick and the introduction of a Flemish Renaissance tower give the composition a certain vitality. Unfortunately, the much buttressed chapel with its pretty spire was never built. Between 1904-78 the building was used as a teacher training college.

Throughout the 19th century, Hereford City Council met in unpretentious surroundings adjoining the retail markets, on the corner of Widemarsh Street and Maylord Street. As they only met monthly and had few full-time officials, an elaborate setting was unnecessary. Occasionally, for important functions, the Old Town Hall in High Town was used, but this was basically a market hall-cum-shirehall and, after its demolition in 1861, the City Council merely refurbished its Widemarsh Street premises. But as parliamentary legislation in the late 19th century increased the responsibilities of local authorities, the Council began to discuss the possibility of erecting a more imposing edifice, to provide a new municipal focus for the City. In 1900 the City Surveyor, John Parker, who had earlier displayed his architectural skill with the Broomy Hill water tower (1882) and the Victoria Bridge (1897), produced a drawing for a new Town Hall in Widemarsh Street. It shows that baroque revivalism was already the chosen style before H.A. Cheers arrived with the design for the present Town Hall in 1902. Parker's building is far less monumental, but in detail it owes a great deal to the Arts and Crafts movement, while the domed corner-tower is almost a cliché among institutional buildings of this era.

Demonstrating that even in the 19th century Hereford was still the capital of the southern marches and the adjoining parts of Wales, the Herefordshire and South Wales Eye and Ear Institute was established in the City in July, 1882. But not until 1884 were premises, with room for five beds, acquired in Commercial Road, immediately in front of the Baptist chapel. This early Georgian cottage, with attractive keystones, quoins and a rather nice bracketed hood, soon proved to be inadequate, and in 1889 the Institute moved to the Victoria Hospital in Eign Street. Sadly, the little cottage was demolished.

The Black Lion in Bridge Street, showing its early 17th century bones during restoration in the 1890s. It was soon to be plastered over again and not permanently exposed until 1974. For all their romanticism, the Victorians generally had a down-to-earth attitude to functional timber-framed buildings. The Black Lion has been here for a long time, for the Royal Commissioners detected an earlier stone building in 1931 — perhaps the house with a stone chamber that belonged in the Middle Ages to the monks of Dore Abbey. Upstairs, discovered by accident in 1932, is the finest room of its period in Hereford — the Commandment Room with panelling, overmantel, a plaster ceiling enriched with foliage and vases, and a series of näive wall paintings, dating from the 16th century, which depict seven of the ten commandments — adultery is especially memorable. In the 19th century the Black Lion was described as 'an agricultural inn'.

When this photograph was taken before the First World War, Pool Farm in Belmont Road was still a working farm. It belonged to Francis Millichamp, who grazed the well-watered pasture lands which stretched down behind the house to the Wye, and grew corn across the road in White Cross Field and Walnuttree Field situated in the wedge of land between the roads to Ross and Abergavenny. Beneath the brick and stone facade of the house, there are the remains of an open hall dating from the 15th century. It was sub-divided and ceiled with great moulded beams in the mid-16th century by the Wilcox family. James Wilcox also built the porch, which is dated 1624, after a struggle with the City Council, who regarded it as an encroachment upon the main road. The farm just avoided demolition in the 1970s — a fate which overtook its neighbour Causeway Farm, on the right of the photograph. It is now well restored but — alas — the beautiful wisteria has disappeared.

CENTRE

There was great excitement in the City in May 1919 when an internal chimney collapsed at the Booth-hall Inn, exposing the elaborate 15th century roof of the hall used by the merchant guild of Hereford in the Middle Ages. How such a remarkable example of mediaeval carpentry, with its complicated mouldings, beautifully carved figures, great windbraces and delicate foiled openings could be 'lost' is difficult to explain. It probably occurred when the hall was leased in the 18th century. The building was then said to be 'ruinous and in great decay'. To-day it can be viewed in something like its original condition.

RIGHT

A late 19th century photograph, showing the remains of the Chapter House of Hereford Cathedral. This mound of rubble was all that remained of the reputedly earliest fan vault in England, built by the mason Thomas of Cambridge between 1364-71. The roof of the building was apparently removed during the Civil War, while Bishop Blisse (1712-21) pulled down two windows and some walling to restore his palace. Finally, in 1769, because of its dangerous condition, the Dean and Chapter had no alternative but to order its demolition. It remained an informal quarry until 1937, when the area was tidied up by the Friends of the Cathedral, creating one of the most sublime spots in the City — highly recommended as a place to ponder upon the mysteries of the world on warm summer days.

BELOW

The Blackfriars cloister, photographed in 1924 before its restoration. The Dominicans arrived in Hereford in 1246, but so encumbered was the City with religious foundations, Pope Innocent IV prohibited their settlement. Their first attempt at founding a friary in the Portfields was frustrated by the canons of the Cathedral, who demolished the building and carried off the materials for their own use. Eventually, through the good offices of Bishop Cantilupe, they acquired a site next to the hospital of St John in Widemarsh Street, where they built a large church, now under the Aylestone School playground, and the cloister shown here. After the Dissolution, the property was purchased by the Coningsbys of Hampton Court who used the stone in 1614 to build the present almshouses. The cloister was retained and converted into a town house. This was probably destroyed and abandoned during the Civil War, when the Whitemarsh suburb was levelled to improve the security of the City, by the Royalist governor Barnabus Scudamore. By the 18th century the building was much as it appears in this photograph.

On Friday, 28 June 1901 a 'large company' gathered at a new 'smart hotel' in Widemarsh Street as guests of Mr and Mrs Clay, lately host and hostess of the Coach and Horses in Commercial Street. The occasion was to mark the opening of a 'beautiful specimen of half-timbered domestic gothic of the late 15th century type'. The architect was G.H. Godsell, whose abilities, according to the *Hereford Journal,* were 'too well known locally to need recapitulation'. What a pity, for here was an architect of considerable talent who produced the first — and finest — piece of vernacular revivalism to grace Hereford's ancient streetscape. Godsell was associated with one of the best Victorian church architects, James Brooks — a friend of William Morris — and with him submitted a scheme for the new Town Hall in St Owen Street. Sadly, perhaps, it was runner-up to the winning design.

ECHOES OF ANTIQUITY

ABOVE

Few other cities in England engaged in the fashionable game of 'improvement' with such zeal as Hereford in the late 18th and early 19th centuries. Like many recent councils, the City fathers believed that, by making Hereford's streets 'airy', 'neat' and 'uniform', the City would enjoy an era of prosperity unparalleled since the 13th century. Happily for us, the spectre of the Industrial Revolution remained a grey cloud on the eastern and south-western horizons. Nevertheless, a great deal of Hereford's character was sacrificed in anticipation of its arrival, including the wall, gates, narrow streets, timber-framed buildings, Market Hall and St Nicholas's Church. This venerable pile, first mentioned in the 12th century, occupied a delightfully inconvenient spot in front of the Orange Tree in King Street. From a vignette on Taylor's plan it seems to have undergone extensive restoration c1700, when it was provided with a rather Islamic porch and classical windows. The chancel, however, was still romanesque. This pencil sketch was made on the eve of its demolition in 1842. The broad-wheeled waggon was perhaps included to suggest how securely the church plugged one of the main thoroughfares of the City. To-day only a depression in the building line — and, of course, a small carpark — marks where it stood.

INSET

'A capital from St Nicholas' Church at the rear of a house now demolished in Broad Street' — according to the legend on Alfred Watkin's photograph. This rather finely moulded octagonal base seems to date from the 15th century, although the capital, with traces of a primitive stiff leaf, may perhaps be two centuries earlier.

BELOW

At the end of the 18th century, the City Wall was virtually intact; the gates had gone, but it was still possible to perambulate the defences beside the wet ditch along what was known as the 'sally walk', after the willows that grew there. In June 1784 Viscount Torrington made a circuit of the City 'where the ancient wall and turrets continue, not very dilapidated'. The draining of the ditch in the 1850s rang the death knell of the wall, as many more sub-standard houses and buildings were erected against its outer face. In many places the wall disappeared completely, and only re-emerged on occasions such as this, when the Wellington Inn on the corner of Widemarsh Street was rebuilt c1895. The large blocks of ashlar stone suggest that this was a stretch of the original 13th century wall, rather than a subsequent rebuild. The warehouse behind still stands in Wall Street, overlooking the Ring Road.

A wonderful cross-section of the City Wall, photographed when West Street was pushed through to Victoria Street in 1890. Modern excavations adjoining this site have confirmed Alfred Watkin's pioneering thesis, that the defences of Hereford were constructed in several phases. This section shows the massive turf and clay rampart erected in the age of Alfred, which turned the cathedral City into an urban fortress, and prevented western Britain being swamped by the Vikings. Because of this bank, a way of life survived in this country which was quite different from feudal societies developing on the Continent. Hereford thus contributed to the unique quality of English civilisation. The puny mediaeval wall, erected in the early 13th century, more as a symbol of civic pride than for defence, was at this point simply clamped onto the existing rampart.

RIGHT

A section of the City Wall in Bath Street, exposed during the clearance of sub-standard housing in the 1930s. These Victorian cottages were built in the City ditch, after it had been drained during the improvements of the mid-19th century. By then most of the stone from the wall, which was originally three to four feet thick, had been removed, simply leaving the veneer shown in the photograph, which was useful either as a property boundary or a house wall. A further section of wall pierced with windows can be seen in the distance. Notice also the difference in levels inside and outside the defences. In the Middle Ages the road inside the defences was designed to give easy access for would-be defenders to the wall and its bastions.

BELOW LEFT

Every alley in an historic city can provide a curiosity. Here are the remains of a 14th century bay window lost in a yard behind Broad Street. Presumably, it once threw light into a rich merchant's solar. It has now disappeared, but the photograph provides further evidence of the extensive use of stone for domestic buildings in Hereford during the Middle Ages.

CENTRE RIGHT

For lovers of antiquity there is nothing quite so rewarding as poking around in the suburban shrubberies and rockeries of an ancient city. It is here, more often than not, that the cast-off relics of the past, scraped from the City's monuments by over zealous restorers, finally come to rest. In 1901 Mr Francis Merrick of Goodrich House (later Waldrist) Venns Lane, seems to have had a fairly comprehensive collection. The cross is reputed to have come from the Whitecross, but more likely it sat on the gable end of a City church. There was also the base of a 14th century finial, a clustered column and a grotesque head. The splendid 12th century scalloped capital, serving as a miniature garden, appears to be carved in an oolitic or Caen stone and may perhaps have formed part of the romanesque work at the Cathedral. Where are these pieces to-day?

BELOW

A low-budget team of City engineers, equipped with horses and sturdy carts, uncover the foundations of a round chapel on the corner of St Owen Street and Ledbury Road in 1927. This had remained hidden but not forgotten in folk-memory, beneath the rectangular chapel of St Giles' Hospital, built in 1692, which had just been dismantled and re-erected on its present site. Like the round church discovered at Garway in the same year, this chapel belonged to the Templars, who had established a hospital here in the mid-12th century. The faded tympanum, depicting the Good Shepherd, now set in the wall of the almshouses, which dates from c1150, was probably situated over the doorway of this chapel. Some of the stones can still be seen on the corner, but the rest were sacrificed to the motor car.

An exciting find behind Mr Beeson's veterinary surgery at 145 St Owen Street — a complete 15th century fireplace, beautifully finished with moulded pilasters, capitals and stepped lintels. How many other fairly ordinary buildings in Hereford still hide antiquities such as this?

In March 1934 the Freeman's Prison, which occupied a yard to the west of the Booth-hall, was demolished and Hereford lost a fine early 16th century building. The photograph shows the ground floor, with its elaborately moulded bressemer and matching cross-beams, which were painted and inscribed with letters. There was a plaster ceiling with *fleur de lys* motifs, panelling on the walls and a contemporary bay window. The prison was used by the burgesses of the City who, protected by their charters, were immune from prosecution in the county courts. This richly appointed building shows that the freemen-felons expected to live in some style, even in prison.

Few people realise that beneath the modern facades of High Town there are structures of considerable antiquity. This barge-board was removed from the rear of No 20 — now Stead and Simpson — in 1920. The boldly executed vine-trail, with its crisp leaves and succulent stems, dates from the 15th century and is reminiscent of the foliage carved on the rood screens at Moreton on Lugg and Pipe and Lyde. Beneath the building there is also a four-centred vaulted cellar of approximately the same date. Until the mid-19th century this property was known as the Sun Tavern which, although described as 'newly fitted up' in 1771, was one of the oldest inns in the City. A jolly society called The Association for the Prosecution of Felons met here in the early 19th century, and in 1657 it was the scene of a riot, when two gentry factions battled in the closets and on the staircases, and were only suppressed after a party of soldiers had been called from the Castle.

At Whitfield a single column supporting a byre has an elegant capital and finely moulded profile, which hints to an earlier, more distinguished career as one of the twenty-seven pillars supporting the Old Hereford Town Hall. This building, 'the most fantastic black and white building imaginable', was erected c1550 and, until 1862, stood in High Town. After a good deal of heart searching, it was demolished to ease the flow of traffic through the City. Several of its indestructible timbers together, it seems from the photograph, with their stone plinths, were sold to local landowners.

126

ABOVE

'The last of the Old Red Lion', Eign Street. One of Hereford's most ancient pubs, a glorious multi-gabled building, timber-framed throughout, it stood until 1896 just outside Eign Gate. It was a popular place for auctions and commercial travellers; its success led to a replacement building, equally distinguished but now also gone — only the name remains.

LEFT

In 1931 the Royal Commission on Historical Monuments found 115 domestic buildings in Hereford dating from before 1714. These buildings, along with the more obvious monuments like churches and almshouses, were considered by the Commissioners to be worthy of preservation, because they were illustrative of contemporary culture, civilisation and conditions of life of the people of England from the earliest times. To-day, half a century later, over a quarter of these buildings have disappeared without trace. Almost all of them were timber-framed. This area of Hereford is now a disgrace, and yet it stands within 50 yards of the Cathedral. In 1931, Little Berrington Street was fully peopled and contained examples of minor domestic architecture, ranging from the 15th to 19th centuries. There was even a pub called the Golden Lion. Gradually in the '30s and '40s the houses were condemned and it was cleared out, leaving a vacuum, into which crept an ill-assorted mixture of small industries and car parks. No attempt was made to refurbish these solid-looking 18th century town houses, or to save the interesting mediaeval house in the foreground. The Gloucester Inn can be seen at the top of the street.

CENTRE

Great moulded and socketed timbers are being loaded onto a truck in 1938 as another piece of Hereford's ancient fabric bites the dust. A few years before, the Royal Commission on Historic Monuments had extolled the mid-17th century features of the Gloucester House Inn in Berrington Street, commenting especially upon its interesting staircase with twisted balusters. It was first mentioned in 1712, when the landlord was a carpenter called David Randall, who no doubt provided accommodation for the Gloucester carrier — hence its name. Nothing more graphically demonstrates the changing character of English cities than the demise of the urban inn.

RIGHT

The elderly members of the Hereford Temperance Society, who successfully prevented the City licensees from obtaining an extension of opening hours for Edward VII's coronation in 1902, must have been encouraged by the spate of demolitions in the 1930s, which saw the disappearance of pubs such as the White Horse. The Royal Commission on Historic Monuments regarded the White Horse, which stood on the corner of Gaol Street/Union Street, as a 17th century building, but the arched braces and large square panels suggest an earlier date. I wonder how many people in Hereford developed a taste for Wintles Health Ales. It made a change, no doubt, from Messrs Watkins & Co's Golden Sunlight. In 1857 the White Horse was called the Flower Pot.

ABOVE

Two buildings worthy of preservation, mid-way along the south side of Eign Gate but swept away in the mid-1960s; not good enough at that date to be squeezed into the grade II category of buildings of special architectural interest, albeit basically 17th century and timber-framed. Now that Eign Gate has been pedestrianised, the strong gabled profile of the Barrell Vaults and its neighbour would have enriched the present rather repetitive streetscape. The smaller towns of Herefordshire, especially Kington and Ledbury, still retain many buildings like these, with grey rendered facades which almost epitomise the 19th century town.

LEFT

The host and hostess of the Bowling Green Inn, Bewell Street pose before their business in 1912. In this year the magistrates challenged the renewal of their licence on the grounds that the premises were structurally unsound, the rooms were small and ventilation poor — the perfect public house atmosphere. Their architect, Mr H. Skyrme, in mitigation explained that the City Council had indicated its intention to widen Bewell Street by seventeen feet, but had failed to produce concrete plans. It was not until c1935 that the pub was finally re-built — set back with room for the largest lorries. The pub was originally attached to its namesake — the bowling green — and was a favourite place for meetings. The Palladian Lodge of the Masons was founded here in 1762, as was the Society for the Prosecution of Felons in 1824.

RIGHT

A magnificent piece of timber-framing situated at the top end of Bewell Street, underbuilt on the ground floor, but jettied above, with a fine moulded bressumer which provides an early 16th century date for construction. The doors giving access to the street above ground level are reminiscent of quayside buildings, perhaps Amsterdam or Antwerp, and suggest warehousing, but at the time the photograph was taken it was occupied by George Stanley, a hairdresser. The date 1909 can be read on the auctioneer's notice which refers to the sale of 'three cottages', Nos 2, 3 and 4 Bewell Street. Soon after the First World War the building was demolished — a great loss.

These low antique cottages, so obviously timber-framed beneath their rendering, were demolished in 1901 to make way for the new Town Hall. The property on the right was given as a gift to the City by the daughters of Richard Johnson, Town Clerk from 1832-68, but the 1,220 sq yards of ground space was inadequate for a new municipal building, offering, in the words of John Parker, City Surveyor 'little scope for a dignified elevation'. As a result the YWCA, who occupied the adjoining premises, were persuaded to move across the street to a purpose-built hostel — the Percival Hall. A.H. Cheers, the architect of the Town Hall, insisted that the 'fine old panelling' in the YWCA building be preserved. To-day it still enhances Committee Room No 1. The rest disappeared, including a splendid studded 17th century door with flanking console brackets. Hereford gained a monument but lost a little more character.

LEFT

Two pretty, but rather sub-standard cottages, situated somewhere in Hereford c1900. Although it is difficult to substantiate, they probably stood in one of the lanes which stretched from Bewell Street to Wall Street — Bewell Court, Weaver's Alley, Sheriff's Court, Fryer's Court and Portman's Alley. They were cleared out in 1907 under the Housing of the Working Classes Act 1890, and it seems likely that W.H. Bustin, who recorded most of the important events of this era, would bring his camera here. The lack of perspective suggests a cramped alley. In the schedule of demolition the cottages are described as 'of great age', but the arrangement of the frames, lattice windows with irregular glass and the square headed doors, makes it most likely that they were erected in the late 17th century. Restored and occupied, they would have made a splendid foil for the new architecture of the Tesco store.

CENTRE

The studded and battened door of No 136 St Owen Street. These bold brackets enriched with acanthus, are typical products of Welsh Border craftsmanship in the Jacobean era. Ultimately, the scrolls derive from the volutes of the Ionic Order, which first appears in Herefordshire in the 1570s but by the early 17th century had been well digested. Similar Renaissance ornamentation, executed with barbarian gusto, occurs on the Old House, the building in High Street and the porch of the Farmer's Club in Widemarsh Street.

RIGHT

A mutilated Ceres, the goddess of plenty, stands silent witness to the desecration of William Startin's Corn Exchange in Broad Street c1936. For thirty years longer, 'The Farmers Toll Free Corn Exchange' survived, without its clock tower, as the Kemble Theatre. The foundation stone for the Exchange was laid on 9 May 1857 by Lady Emily Foley, on the site of Hereford's first theatre which, according to a contemporary description, was 'a remarkable small and ill-supported erection'. In 1908, however, a piece of land at the rear of the Exchange was purchased, and the auditorium of the Kemble Theatre was created and 'dedicated to the advancement of what is pure in literature, elevating in art, inspiring in morals and innocent in amusement'. Sadly, these aspirations were quietly forgotten in 1963, when the building was demolished and replaced with offices.

BELOW

Not a rural scene in deepest Herefordshire but the garden of Miss Johnson and Mrs Glynn, daughters of the Town Clerk, Richard Johnson who left this house at 136 St Owen Street to the City. The building, with its single gable and clustered chimneys, appears to date from the 17th century and, when the site was cleared for the new Town Hall, architect Mr Cheers insisted that all the materials of value should be stored, some to be used in the new building. The overflowing and viridescent garden is especially lyrical. To-day it is difficult to imagine that this stood within a few yards of the hub of the City.

FIRE AND FLOOD

ABOVE AND CENTRE

At 1.00 am on Tuesday, 9 April 1889 the Yazor Brook burst its banks at Canon Moor and Widemarsh, inundating over 100 houses in Millbrook Street, Newtown Road and Widemarsh Street. A rather lugubrious report in the *Hereford Journal* is relieved by a description of the inhabitants of these areas, jumping out of bed to 'save their bacon', ie rescuing their pigs from drowning. At the Coningsby Hospital the water rushed through the courtyard and out at the back, past the ruins of the Blackfriars. When morning came, northern Hereford, from Widemarsh to the Ledbury Road, was one gigantic lake. The water, seeking the lowest ground, followed the railway line through Barton and debouched into the Wye meadows from two spectacular falls on either side of the embankment leading to Hunderton Bridge. For 36 hours the station was closed and a ferry service was arranged, to carry signal men and passengers to Barrs Court. 'Barton Station' reports the *Journal,* 'seldom has a remarkably attractive appearance, but the whole scene, with the trucks in the siding half hidden in the torrent, with no engine to be seen, the signal boxes untenanted, standing like deserted lighthouses was a most desolate one'. Three years later the Midland Railway Company closed the passenger station.

LEFT

On 23 February 1895, the *Hereford Journal,* with its usual attention to detail, described the dedication of the new chancel of St Martin's Church, Ross Road. The architects were Nicholson and Sons and the work was paid for by Mr & Mrs Hutchinson of the Poole, Belmont Road. The rest of the building, erected in 1845 — 'neither better nor much worse than the generality of churches built at that period' — was suitably enriched and completely restored by Messrs Beavan & Hodges. The following day, just after lunch, almost as if the Almighty disapproved of the work, a mighty gale blew 16 feet off the top of the spire, depositing it in the children's gallery, 'pulverising the seats'. Fortunately, the church was empty, but elsewhere in Hereford builders were blown from scaffolding, slates from St Peter's School bombarded pedestrians in Bath Street, chimneys fell, eight trees in the avenue at Green Crize were uprooted and such was the turbulence on the Wye, rail traffic crossing Hunderton Bridge was drenched with spray.

RIGHT

A familiar scene in St Martin's on Thursday, 15 November 1895, with the Wye 16ft 6ins above its summer level. In the vivid language of the *Hereford Journal* 'a wild waste of water' presented itself from the Castle Green while St Martin's Street had 'the appearance of a canal', making 'pedestrian traffic quite out of the question'. Apparently, an enterprising citizen brought out his pony and four wheeler and — for a fee — began ferrying stranded passengers. After continuous rain from Sunday evening, the flood water reached a peak at 6.00 am on Thursday, and was already receding when this photograph was taken. The cameraman, Mr Bustin, referred to himself in contemporary advertisements as 'an Artist Photographer' — hence, perhaps, the acrobatic boy on the lamp post. To-day all the buildings on the right and in the middle distance — which included a fine early 16th century timber-framed range — have disappeared, to be replaced by a fuel oil depôt and a traffic island.

The Victoria suspension bridge with the floodwater lapping over its approaches on Tuesday, 27 August 1912. The summer of 1912 was the wettest since records began in Herefordshire in 1818. Between June and August, 49 inches of rain had fallen and, as a measure of the dismal conditions, only 14 bathers were received at the Bartonsham bathing station between 17 and 31 August, when at that time of the year several hundred were usually recorded each week. The weather reached its nadir on Tuesday, 27 August when, at 1.00 pm, the Wye was 14ft 10ins above its summer level. Hereford was an island. The inhabitants of Mortimer Road, Newtown Road and Edgar Street were urged by the Council to move their pigs and fowls to higher ground, and the road to Worcester was flooded on the Lugg causeway. Worst of all, the county cricket match scheduled for Widemarsh Common between Herefordshire and East Gloucestershire was postponed. The rain stopped in the late afternoon and gave way to a clear moonlit night, 'one of the few lately experienced', which brought many house-weary citizens onto Wye Bridge and Castle Cliffe to enjoy the 'luminous light thrown across the expansive waters'. It was apparently 'a sight worth seeing'.

The brothers Jordan — and daughters — out of work and disconsolate about the wettest summer on record. The damp patch on the pontoon suggests their dogs, unlike the Bartonsham bathers, were undeterred by the weather and prepared to take a dip.

ABOVE

Jordan's boats and pontoon on a better day but still not busy; above on the bank with finial, bay window and gothick corner tower, the terminus building of the Hereford and Abergavenny tramway.

LEFT

On a dismal day c1930, spectators gathered around a stranded Foden steam lorry at Drybridge. The steam and smoke still gushes from the engine's boiler after a frantic struggle to release it from its watery pit. The vehicle belonged to the Imperial Flour Mills in Friar Street and was obviously carrying a heavy load of Watkin's Flour — 'unequalled for flavour' — when it stumbled upon the subterranean stream which is clearly shown on the earlier maps of the City. In the Middle Ages it was crossed by the 'Suthbrugge of Hereford' which, because of the seasonal nature of the stream, subsequently became Drybridge — clearly a misnomer on this occasion. The dull weather also produced difficulties for the photographer, Walter Pritchard, hence the booted ghost beside the engine and the blurred features of one of the bystanders. What a difference the creeper makes to the austere but familiar walls of Drybridge House in the background.

RIGHT AND BELOW

At 3.30 am on Monday, 23 December 1901 the residents of Green Street were rudely awoken by a loud explosion, which ripped the roof from St James's Church. A few minutes earlier a sleepy nurse on night duty at the General noticed an unusual light across the yard at the rear of the hospital, and wisely sent an urgent message to the fire station in Gaol Street. It was an intensely cold night and as the 'plucky' firemen retired after making strenuous efforts to subdue the flames, their water-sodden uniforms froze. Within two hours, it was all over and as Christmas Eve dawned, Hereford's prettiest 19th century church 'resembled the ruins of the world famed Tintern Abbey'. Several members of the Evensong congregation remembered how warm the church had felt the night before and, as a result, the blame was laid upon the recently installed gas burners. A less generous correspondent in the paper saw divine retribution at work upon a building which broke the sacred traditions of the Christian church by having a north-western chancel. Later in the day a shocked parish meeting learnt from the vicar that the building was not insured. As the editorial of the *Hereford Journal* thundered: 'Someone has clearly blundered'. Within two years the church was restored — the chancel still faces NW.

IN TIME OF WAR

LEFT

The Welsh Border Brigade bearer company, with all eyes not to the front, photographed at the Militia Barracks in Harold Street in 1902. The occasion was probably the visit of Princess Henry of Battenberg to Hereford on 13 May, when the streets of the City were lined with soldiers. Later, at the Town Hall, the Princess presented medals to the volunteers who had served in the South African War. A tablet in the Cathedral records the men from Herefordshire who died serving with the Welsh Border Brigade.

BELOW

When war broke out in 1914 the civilian population of Hereford, especially the middle classes, imbued with a spirit of self-help and not a little jingoism, were eager to support the struggle across the Channel. Although the press constantly attacked 'slackers', the army had more recruits than it could train, at least until the end of 1916. Unaware of this, however, throughout the summer of 1915, garden parties were held to raise funds for the Voluntary Training Corps — a kind of Home Guard intended to relieve the regular and territorial army of home duties. After a fête held at the Vineyard Croft in August, £71 14s was raised, which bought 15 rifles, bugles and bayonets for the 150-strong Hereford corps. As the war progressed and conscription was introduced, the *raison d'etre* of the Voluntary Corps was questioned. It was suggested by some unkind correspondents that they should be sent to France to dig trenches.

RIGHT

In August 1915, while money was being raised for their support at the Vineyard Croft, the Herefordshire Volunteers were camping at Monnington-on-Wye. Virtually all their equipment was supplied by Hereford firms, including a generous ration of cider by Messrs Bulmer & Co. The quartermaster was George Holloway, proprietor of the Exchange and Mart Furniture Warehouse in Commercial Street, who presumably supplied the mattresses which the happy campers are stuffing with straw, observed by a curious and rather satanic cook.

When Count Louis Bodenham-Lubienski died in 1912 the Rotherwas estate, totalling 2,577 acres, was auctioned as 76 separate lots. Thus, a major gentry estate with a continuous history, at least from the 15th century, vanished for ever. An attempt was made to utilise the mansion as a 'hydro' but this failed, and in 1913 the superb Renaissance interior was stripped from the house and sold separately. It is now at Amherst College, Massachusetts. The County Council bought 185 acres of the estate lying towards Lower Bullingham for smallholdings — a use for which they proved to be most unsatisfactory because of flooding. In 1916, with Lloyd George as Minister of Munitions, the Council was temporarily relieved of its white elephant by the Government, eager to disperse armament production into the countryside. In September, the same month that the paper reported the death of Count Lubienski's eldest son and heir, Lieut H.E.C. Bodenham, the Government's proposals were revealed to Hereford. Within six months a vast complex of modern prefabricated buildings had mushroomed beneath Dinedor Hill and, by the end of 1917, between 5-6,000 women were employed at the National Filling Factory — as it was known locally.

The arrival late in 1916 of hundreds of single girls, from the industrial cities of the Midlands and the North, threatened to produce a serious social problem for Hereford. Not least, according to a correspondent in the *Hereford Times,* because they would corrupt the decent yeomen of the county — those, that is, who were lucky enough not to be fighting in Flanders. Seen here posed on a footbridge at Rotherwas like some Atlantaean phalanx, with their puny foremen, they certainly seem harmless enough. The Mother Huff caps were worn to prevent static electricity, which was apparently a rather lethal problem for a shell-filler. Finding suitable accommodation was another difficulty, albeit the Mayor regularly appealed in the newspaper for lodgings, stressing that the munition worker was 'in the truest sense fighting our battles'. Following an acrimonious debate about absentee canons, a number of Roman Catholic girls were provided with wardened accommodation at The Residence in Broad Street.

The military police at the Royal Ordnance Factory in 1918. The basic role of the corps was to maintain the internal and external security of the establishment and, although the enemy ignored the factory, the presence of so many women created its own problems. Much of their time was spent searching inmates for cigarettes and matches and, occasionally, this led to an explosive situation, as in October 1917, when a female worker was sentenced to one month's hard labour for assaulting a policeman. An attempted strike in 1917, when some of the workers armed themselves with red flags and broomsticks, also created friction. The police are photographed here in front of their HQ — an elegant piece of Wrenish architecture whose permanence suggests that the Government expected the War to last a long time.

On Sunday, 7 September 1919, Hereford paid its tribute to those who had fallen in the Great War. Close to a temporary cenotaph erected in High Town, several thousand people attended a drum-head service conducted by the Bishop of Hereford, Herbert Hensley Henson. Letters of comfort were received and read from the King, Queen Alexandra and Field Marshal Earl Haig, and the Bishop's 'inspiring address' was printed in full in the *Hereford Times.* Not everyone in Hereford was mourning on that day, for when the pubs closed a drunk stumbled across High Town and spat on the floral tributes clustered beneath the monument — much to the disgust of a lady letter-writer in the *Times* the following week.

ILLUSTRATIONS

INDEX

SUBSCRIBERS

Presentation Copies

1 Hereford District Council
2 County Council of Hereford & Worcester
3 Hereford Library
4 County Records office, Hereford
5 Hereford College of Further Education

6 David Whitehead
7 Clive & Carolyn Birch
8 Stephen & Victoria Wegg-Prosser
9 Wegg-Prosser
10 Janet Sheehan
11 Mrs M. Purcell
12 G. Exley
13 P. Wilson
14 Mrs H. Bailey
15 Miss M. Fielden
16 Mrs Adams
17 Mrs J. Powell
18 William Purser
19 Mrs M.F. Powell
20 A.K. Beese
21 D.S. Southey
22 Bernard F. Joss
23 Mrs N. Walters
24 Mrs A.N Powell
25 Mr & Mrs G.B. Jones
26 Mrs J. Slade
27 Bishop of Hereford's Bluecoat School
28 Rev W.I.O. McDonald
29 Mrs K.J. Davies
30 Chris Davies
31 A.G. Welch
32 Mrs G.M.C. Mitchell
33 R.N.L. Denyer
34 A.V. Ryder
35 G.C. Cartwright
36 Peter Chard
37 A.E. Alakija
38 Ursula Marion Mills
39 Victoria & Albert Museum
40 Mr & Mrs W.A. Gardner
41 Nicholas Handoll
42 Mr & Mrs R.L. Hancorn
43 Mr & Mrs S.J. Hancorn
44 Miss J.E. Davies
45 G.H. Burdge
46 B. Weekes
47 Royal National College for the Blind
48 Mr & Mrs I.J. Broom
49 Mrs J.S. Morris
50 Mrs J.E. Austin

51 Ian Williams
52 H.G. Culliss
53 Miss N. Bell
54 Miss E.M. Wheeldon
55 Dr. W.H.J. Baker
56 Betty M. Joyce
57 R.J. Nash
58 Derek Foxton
59 K.A. Carey
60 Anne Sandford
61 Hereford City Museum
62 Mr & Mrs N. Dees
63 P.J. Draper
64 Hereford Technical College
65 C.R. Randall
66 Mrs B.D. Kelly
67 Mrs Speight
68 Mrs S.R. Phillips
69 E.R. Wood
70 Mr & Mrs J.M. Acheson
71 R.M. Opie
72 G.S. Griffiths
73 M.J.P. McCarthy
74 Mr & Mrs J.M. Acheson
75 Mrs M.A. Baskerville
76 B.J. Watkins
77 M. Whitwell
78 Mrs Fay Smith
79 Graham Roberts
80 Mrs M.H. Brook
81 C.E. Attfield
82 T. Batho
83 Allan Southworth
84 Mrs M. Dando
85 M.E.M. Lloyd
86 Mrs A. Berry Ottaway
87 F.E. Winter
88 C.T. Winter
89 City of Hereford Tourist Information Centre
90 C.T. Ballard
91 Mrs M.H. Brook
92 Mr & Mrs R.L. Hancorn
93 Basil Butcher
94 Mr & Mrs F.C. Buckle
95 Miss M. Slatter

96 E.H. Dorrell
97 D.C. Layton
98 D. Jukes
99 Mrs M. Watkins
100 Mrs R. Williams
101 K.R. Anscomb
102
103 Mrs H. Thomas
104
105 Mrs R.M. Smith
106 G. Rizzardini
107 J.W. Martin
108 Mrs E. Salter
109 H. Williamson
110 Mrs J.H. Ross
111 Mr & Mrs G. Hoskins
112 K.W. Francis
113 R.P. Lowry
114 E.J. Godwin
115 C. Reed
116 Mrs M. Field
117 K.H.J. Pritchard
118 R.A.L. Preece
119 Mrs E.E. Williams
120 M.J. Pavey
121 C.O. Owens
122 A.J. Whiting
123 Bernard Mitchell
124 Mrs J. Ingram
125 A.E. Merritt
126 Mrs Howard
127 Mrs D.A. Davey
128 J.E.C. Farmer
129 S.G.J. Webb
130 Miss M.G. Fenner
131 A. Heston
132 R. Heston
133 W.A. Hart
134 Mrs S.M. Pope
135 R.W.J. Powell
136 Mrs J.M. Gwilliam
137 Mrs E.E. Collins
138 J.R.W. Thomas
139 Mrs M.M.B. Hughes
140 Jean A. Harrop
141 A.P. Jancy
142 Mrs N.P. Jones
143 K.E. Clark
144 R.J. Hayward
145 Mrs V. Vaughan-Jones
146 Mrs C.A. Steele

147 Mrs D.M. Smart
148 T.J.H. Higgins
149 J.C. Boylan
150 R.A. Sockett
151 V. & C. Rosser
152 Ray Boddington
153 Joe Hillaby
154 M.W. Burgess
155 P. England
156 Elaine D. Andrews
157 Mrs A. Thomas
158 Mrs N. Garrett
159 S.L. Beaumont
160 W.G. Davies
161 Mrs J. Collins
162 A.C. Collins
163 Miss E. Monica Jones
164 C.N. Greenland
165 Mr & Mrs K. Paulo
166 Tony Carr
167 Mr & Mrs P.J. Jones
168 A.V. Wood
169 Mrs M. Bradley
170 A. Dickinson
171 M.A. Townsend
172 D.K. Powell
173 Mr & Mrs D.B. Powell
174 Helen Margaret Steel
175 John Edwin Lewis
176 Sally Johnson
177 Mrs G.M. Young
178 Herbert Simmons
179 Mrs M. Stuart
180 S.W. & M.E. Harris
181 Mrs Janet Weaver
182 Miss M.E. Wiles
183 F.E. Skinner
184 Mrs J. Willmont
185 Frank W. Smith
186 Mrs E. Broome
187 Greg Unwin
188 M.W.D. Jones
189 Gillian Murray
190 Mrs E.M. Aylett
191 V.P. Helme
192 Gerald Young
193 Mrs C.M. Powell
194 E.M. Lawrence
195 Mrs I. Mahoney
196 A.J. Rudge
197 A.M. Sims

198 Sandra Thomas	247 D.F. Thomas	300 County Museum	354 Roy Eastwood
199 Mrs J.I. Rutherford	248 B.W. Waters	301 Rev P.L.S. Barrett	355 C. Young
200 S. Roberts	249 N.C. Reeves	302 Major H.J. Lloyd-Jon	356 W.L. Friday
201 G.E. Morris	250 P. & L. Bradburn	OBE, TD, LLD,	357 A.H. Cousins
202 C.J. Greaves	251 Mrs J.M. Heygate	FSA	358 L.C. Jones
203 J. Harden BSc	252 E.G. Shankie	303 A.V. Ryder	359 B.F. Croker
204 Roy Massey	253 Mr & Mrs P.J. Wride	304 Mrs J.M. Briffett	360 D. Potter
205 Mrs G.S. Troth	254 M.T. Anderson	305 P.J. Jones	361
206 T.A. Jones	255 Mrs K.M. Milne	306 J.S. Steward	362 Mrs M. Hale
207 Wellington County	256 B.R. Freeman	307 Gillian Murray	363 Mrs G. Bradshaw
Primary School	257 Hunderton Junior	308 Dr J. Lane	364 K. Taylor
208 Shirley Monger	School	309 Mrs P.H. Lees-Smith	365 Mrs B.J. Morris
209 Aeroparts Engineering	258 S.L. Beaumont	310 D.E. Williams	366 Mrs R.E. Bridges
Co Ltd	259 Mary Sophia Watkins	311 R. Peek	367 K.L. Brown
210 Counter Caterers Ltd	260 Mrs J.I. Rutherford	312 Geo Wilkins	368 Mrs M. Carter
211 Lacy Evans	261 J.R. Setterfield	313 P.J.H. Mort	369 Alan Street
212 Blake & Son (Hereford)	262 N. Keeble	314 S. Brinded	370 Mrs I.I. Hoddell
Ltd	263 Mrs J.B. Lambert	315 S. & V. Webb	371 Mrs A. Vaughan
213 M.S. Davis	264 Mrs E.M. Rees	316 J.E. Dunn	372 Mr & Mrs L.G. Caswell
214 Geo Wilkins	265 R. Shoesmith	317 S.W. Smith	373 M.T. Hemming
215 Ronald Peek	266 M. Colman	318 J.R. Setterfield	374 Ann Fishlock
216 D.E. Williams	267 G. Charnolk	319 Sally Johnson	375 Miss B. Arbuckle
217 R.S. Halls	268 Scott Brinded	320 Mrs C.J.C. Renton	376 K. Lewis
218 Mrs Ann Davey	269 A.J. Weston	321 B.V.C. Stone	377 Mrs V. Owen
219 B.V.C. Stone	270 Dr R.S. Hall	322 G.W. Smith	378 Group Captain J.B.
220 Alan Stewart	271 Herefordshire Technic	323 P. Charleton	Lewis
221 R.J. Williams	College	324 Mrs P.J. Clarke	379 H.E. Godfrey
222 John M. Williams	272 Mrs K.J. Watkins	325 Mrs C.N. Greenland	380 A. Matthews
223 Ivor Whittal-Williams	273 A.B. Sherratt	326 E. Prosser	381 D. Scott
224 Mrs E.M. Williams	274 Mrs J.M. Bentley-	327 A.P. Drabble	382 Mrs Amott
225 Roy Massey	Taylor	328 N.J. Robinson	383 S.G. Lawrence
226 Gillian Bulmer	275 Charles Renton	329 Mrs M.J.G. Jenkins	384 P.C. Cooper
227 Mrs W.J. Hoddell	276 J.G. Sweetman	330 G.J. Young	385 Mrs J. Cooper
228 Wing Cdr A.M. Gill,	277 John Taylor	331 Mrs M.H. Holliday	386 G.N. Matthews
OBE, DFC, AE,	278 Josephine Mary Rogers	332 G.J. Holliday	387 Mrs S. Watkins
FRAeS, MIPM,	279 Agnes Rogers	333 N.M. & S. Heins	388 Major Robert James
MBIM	280 W.H. Phillips	334 Mrs J. Sockett	Hereford
229 C.J. Over	281 Hereford EDC Library	335 A.S. Hughes	389 Major James Newton
230 K. & M. Paulo	282 S.C. Stanford	336 E.H. Clark	Hereford
231 Stanley W. Smith	283 E. Phillips	337 M.M. Cooper	390 Ron & Sheila Parrott
232 Hugh & Jean Phillips	284 D. Apperley	338 Gay Fernyhough	391 Mrs Valerie Magness
233 Sally Julia Lewis	285 M.A. Handford	339 P.J. Tanswell	392 H.W. Evans
234 G.E. Jenkins	286 F.M. Symonds	340 B. Harrison	393 Hereford County
235 Mary Burnett Breen	287 N.S. Carter	341 E.M. Wood	Library
236 Robert E. Deeley	288 D.J. Collins	342	432 H. Dance
237 John C. Keely	289 Dominic Williams	343 B.F. Parker	433 Marshall & Jan Wilson
238 Leslie E. Hyde	290 Adam Williams	344 R. Hudson	434 Jim & Muiriel Tonkin
239 Powys County Library	291 Muriel E. John	345 Mrs M. Penny	435 A.W. Morris
240 C. Penford	292 J.L. Hackman	346 Mrs J.E. Peake	436 Margaret & Barry
241 H.G. Pitt	293 R.H. Davies	347 Mrs H. Pritchard	Watkins
242 G.W. Smith	294 C.E. Walmsley	348 Mrs E. Crisp	437 Mr Gearing
243 Mr & Mrs J.	295 Mrs S. Croasdell	349 C.R. Colley	438 Mrs G.M. Appleton
Zakrzewski	296 J. Taylor	350 Mrs M. Luker	439 A. Cross
244 E.R. Thomas	297 S. Brinded	351 Mrs I.E. Pockett	440 Miss S.J. Burgin
245 E.W. Baynham	298 D. Apperley	352 D.V. Piears	441 E.J. Rowberry
246 P. Charleton	299 J. H. Miners	353 R.E. Wyatt	442 Charles E. Bray
			Remaining names unlisted